# WELSH NOTS, WELSH NOTES
# AND WELSH NUTS

**Abbreviations:**

adj. – *adjective*
A.M. – *Anglo-Manx*
A.W. – *Anglo*-Welsh
Bret. – *Breton*
Corn. – *Cornish*
D.H.S. – *Dictionary of Historical Slang (Partridge)*
G.F.W.I. – *Gwent Federation of Women's Institutes*
G.P.C. – *Geiriadur Prifysgol Cymru*
Gwer. – *Gweriniaethwr ('The Young Republicans')*
hum. – *humorous*
I.G.W. – *'Insight Guide Wales'*
Ir. – *Irish*
Mx. – *Manx*
NWR – *New Welsh Review*
obs. – *obsolete*
Ox. – *Oxford (Dictionary)*
pej. – *pejorative*
R.D.G.E.D. – *Readers Digest Great Encyclopaedic Dictionary*
W. – *Welsh*
W.P.C.S.J. – *The Welsh Pony and Cob Society Journal*

WELSH HERITAGE SERIES – No.8

# Welsh Nots, Welsh Notes and Welsh Nuts

## A *dictionary of phrases using the word 'Welsh*

## T.B. Edwards

# Introduction

It is amazing how many phrases and terms we find in the English language with the word 'Welsh'. Most of us have heard of 'Welsh rabbit' (or 'Welsh rarebit'), the 'Welsh onion' and 'Welsh caviare'. The aim of this book is to present a collection of such phrases. When compiling this list, a line had to be drawn somewhere. Meic Stephens advised me that I should concentrate on the type of entries that 'should be included in Brewer's Dictionary of Phrase and Fable' rather than entries which 'belong to a telephone directory'. Brewer's contains only a few such entries: 'Welsher', 'Welsh cake', 'Welsh harp', 'Welsh main', 'Welsh mortgage' and 'Welsh rabbit' ('Welsh uncle' is also found but under the main entry of 'uncle'). (I have searched for similar phrases and expressions.

The entries have been taken from various topics: food (eg. 'Welshcakes'), folklore (eg. 'Welsh Banshee'), historical terms (eg. 'Welsh Not'), geographical toponyms (eg. 'Welsh Alps' and 'Welsh Athens'), personal epithets (eg. 'Welsh Shakespeare'), music (eg. 'Welsh harp'), dress (eg. 'Welsh wig'), measurements (eg. 'Welsh acre', 'Welsh mile'), furniture (eg. 'Welsh dresser'), breeds of dogs (eg. 'Welsh springer spaniel'), birds (eg. 'Welsh falcon'), other animals (eg. 'Welsh cob' and 'Welsh mountain sheep'), flora (eg. 'Welsh poppy'), religion (eg. 'Welsh Calvinistic Methodists'), politics ('Welsh Nationalist Party'), crafts (eg. 'Welsh love spoon) and many other subjects, even apple varieties (eg. 'Welsh Beauty') etc.

I have not included organisations like the Welsh Hockey Club, yet the 'Welsh Cricket' is here (as it means 'a louse'). Similarly the Welsh Baptists have been omitted yet I have included the Welsh Calvinistic Methodists (Welsh Presbyterians) since they are a distinct denomination. Likewise, while the Welsh Labour Party has been left out, I have mentioned political organisations and societies unique to Welsh history eg. The Welsh Party, The Welsh Language Society, and even the more extreme and eccentric Welsh Distributionist Movement.

It is no coincidence that many terms, as Alan ap Huw observes, are sarcastic and derisive in nature and were coined by the English (1995:11). Obviously insulting examples are 'Welsh bedding' and 'Welsh wife', alluding to the Welshman's/woman's supposed sexuality; or 'Welsh fiddle' depicting the Welshman as dirty. A mean side to the Welsh stereotype can be seen in phrases like 'Welsh bait', while other entries like the 'Welsh comb' try to show the Welshman as unkempt and uncivilized. As Hendrickson says:

'These inhabitants of Wales suffered almost as much abuse at the hands and from the tongues of the English as did the Scottish or Irish. The traditional enemies used "Welsh" to signify anything poor, stupid, or crooked' (1983:220).

Indeed, even the word 'Welsh' itself (from Saxon 'welisc') meant 'foreigner'. Some phrases eg. 'Welsh bean' or 'Welsh nut' can be seen literally as 'foreign' bean or nut and are also for the same reason referred to as 'French bean' or 'French nut', the Frenchman at one time being another much-loathed foreigner.

Whereas the Welsh language is more precise than English in having two words for 'Welsh' – Cymraeg (referring to the Welsh Language) and Cymreig (the adjective for 'Welsh'), the English term 'Welsh' is ambiguous. The word 'Welsh' has a variety of meanings, including a breed of pig, tasteless (of food) in Cambrian dialect and in Scots, it is a surname and as a verb it even has the meaning of not honouring a debt.

Another aspect of linguistic prejudice can be seen in the epithets. While it may no doubt be a great compliment for a Welshman to be described as The Welsh Demosthenes on the Welsh Horace, this tendency to dub great Welsh writers and figures as equivalents of Shakespeare etc. can sometimes be seen in another light. It shows that Welsh achievement has not always been recognised as great for its own merit but patronisingly likened to something/someone else. Thus, as H.T. Edwards writes, in the nineteenth century 'It was galling when

Fleet Street taunted Wales with its want of a Shakespeare, a Milton, a Wordsworth or a Tennyson' (1990:25). While in the musical world Trevor Herbert echoes this when he records that 'from the nineteenth century our boys started being called Handel and Haydn and some were to be called Elgar' (Planet 96:95, Dec./Jan. 1992-3).

Welsh writers themselves have contributed greatly to the source of epithets with the word 'Welsh'. Indeed several entries eg. the Welsh Eldorado and the Welsh Savonarola have come from the pens of individual writers and where possible have been acknowledged. Yet this list is by no means exhaustive. No doubt there are still many other phrases, terms and epithets that lie unnoticed in old Welsh archives. Moreover, writers will always continue to liken Welsh places and people to English or other counterparts. We could well have a Welsh Disneyland one day or oven a Welsh Michael Jackson! Who knows?

*Thornton B. Edwards*
*March 1997*

**Welsh A:** See WELSH MOUNTAIN PONY SECTION A. cf. WELSH PONY SECTION B, WELSH PONY OF COB TYPE SECTION C, WELSH COB SECTION D.

**Welsh a bet:** Not to pay a bet. The verb is 'Welsh' and the culprit a 'Welsher' (qv.). According to Boycott the phrase has nothing to do with a Welshman but rather with a Bob Welch of Epsom 'an English bookie who made off with his bets' (1982:124). cf. WELSH AUCTION, WELSHER.

**Welsh aboriginals:** Robin Wood's term to refer to 'the pre-Celtic inhabitants of Britain, whose Neolithic or Iberian blood is the main ingredient in the British race' (NWR 27:47, Winter 1994/95). See WELSH AUSTRALIAN, WELSH BOOMERANG.

**Welsh Ace,** The: Parry Thomas who died attempting to break a record in 1920's racing his car on Pendine sands. His car was buried in dunes but later exhumed (Sian Llewellyn 1974:27).

**Welsh acre:** 2 English acres (Ox.). In Wales a basic unit of measurement:

| | | |
|---|---|---|
| 4 erw (acres) | = | 1 tyddyn (homestead) |
| 4 tyddyn | = | 1 tref (town) |
| 4 tref | = | 1 maenol (manor) |
| 12 maenol | = | 1 cwmwd (commote) |
| 2 commotes | = | 1 cantref (a Prince's inheritance) |

(see Barnes 1991:154. cf. G.R.J. Jones 1992:95).
In Cornwall a Cornish acre was 120 English acres.
George Owen of Henllys wrote in 1603 that 'The Pembrokeshire acre is four English acres' (Miles ed. 1994:135). Alternatively, according to the length of the 'pole' (into which it was subdivided) 'The Pembrokeshire acre is somewhat less than three English acres' (ibid. p.135). This would make a normal acre similar to a 'stang' (W. Stangell > O.N. stong-pole) which Miles tells us is 'a quarter of a Welsh acre' (1994:306). See WELSH MILE, WELSH YARD.

**Welsh Action United:** See WELSH SOCIALIST VANGUARD.

**Welsh activist:** See WELSH NATIONALIST.

**Welsh-adopted:** Adopted by Wales. Morris, for example, refers to 'Macsen Wledig . . . a Roman-Welsh King – the historical Magnus Maximus, Spanish-born but Welsh-adopted' (1995:30).

**'Welsh Advantage',** The: Motto of the Welsh Development Agency (qv.) used in ford poster.

**Welsh Advisory Council:** Est. 1949 by Labour Party following Welsh nationalist demand for self-government. H.T. Edwards was first chairman.

**Welsh Affairs:** Matters pertaining to Wales.

**Welsh Affairs, Institute of:** (Sefydliad Materion Cymreig).

**Welsh Affairs, Minister for/of:** Cabinet member whose office also includes that of Minister of Housing and Local Government and is responsible for housing policy and town and country planning legislation. He is assisted by the Minister of State for Welsh Affairs.

**Welsh Affairs, Minister of State for:** See WELSH AFFAIRS, MINISTER FOR.

**Welsh Affairs correspondent:** Clive Betts of *The Western Mail.* See WELSH COLUMN.

**Welsh Afternoon:** A unique blend of Welsh tea. cf. WELSH BREAKFAST.

**Welsh Agricultural Show, Royal:** At Builth Wells.

**Welshaholic:** Someone addicted to Welsh language and culture. cf. workaholic. See WELSH-MANIA.

**Welsh Aisle:** Place in St Michael's Church, Oxford where Edward Lhuyd (The Welsh Polymath qv.) is buried in an unmarked grave.

**Welsh 'A' Level:** (Arholiad Lefel/Safon A, Arholiad y gwastad A). 'A' level in Welsh (literature) of which there are two types: for candidates whose mother language is Welsh and for those whose mother tongue is English.

**'Welsh Alcatraz'?:** Maud says of Dolbadarn Castle, Snowdonia that Owain Glyndŵr used it 'as an Alcatraz for his enemy

Reginald Grey of Ruthin' (1994:75). See WELSH COLDITZ.

**Welsh Almanacks:** Category of old Welsh literature (see Elias Owen: 1887: p.v.)

**Welsh Alphabet:** There are 29 letters, including some double letters which are separate letters in Welsh: ch, ff, ll, th. Additionally, after mutations other separate letters are dd and ng. In some Welsh dialects other letters are sh and wh (see Morris 1910). The Alphabet (y Wyddor) was also written in Ogham script (Bethluisnion). A new script called *Coelbren y Beirdd* was devised by Iolo Morganwg. The Ogam alphabet was used also in Ireland and the letters are named after trees.

**Welsh Alps,** The: E.B. in *A Trip to North Wales* (1700) wrote that 'the highest English hills are as cherry stones to the Welsh Alps'. Evan Lloyd also referred to the 'Welsh Alps' in a letter to John Wilkes (1790) (quoted by Stephens, M. ed. 1992 Nos. 298, 383). Snowdonia has also been called the British Alps. Apart from the actual Alps in Europe, there are several non-continental Alps: The Japan Alps and The Southern Alps (in New Zealand) etc. By contrast, the 'Cornish Alps' are the white clay tips in the St Austell region. See WELSH HIGHLANDS, WELSH MATTERHORN, WELSH RABBITS, SOCIETY OF, WELSH SUB-ALPS, WELSH 3,000s, 'WELSH TIGER', THE.

**Welsh Amazons:** 1) The Amazons were the female warriors of Greek mythology. The appellation for Jemima Nicholas and women who on 22nd Feb., 1797 repelled French ships from St David's Head seems well-established. Etheridge talks of 'these Welsh Amazons holding the French at pitchfork point' (1977:25). Roberts cites a description of Jemima Nicholas as 'a tall, stout Amazon masculine woman' (1984:41). Gater also talks of 'Jemima Nicholas and her band of Amazonian warriors' (1991:41). A similar legend concern the Padstow hobby horse, Cornwall whose bright colours likewise repelled a French attack. 2) Thompson refers to the cockle gatherers of Penclawdd as 'these Amazons of the cockle coast' (1937:53).

**Welsh ambassador:** The cuckoo (Ox.). In Welsh 'cog', 'y gog', 'y gwcw'. Waring tells us that 'In Wales . . . it is believed to be unlucky to hear the cuckoo before April 6, but a whole year's prosperity is in store if you hear this for the first time on April 28' (Waring 1978:70). In Risca and Dolwyddelan the people built high hedges to contain the cuckoo, associating it with fine weather – of course, when it was time to leave, the cuckoo flew over the hedges. This is perhaps why J. Green says that a "Welsh ambassador" means 'by extension a fool who poses as wise' (1996:109). See WELSH CORPSE BIRD, WELSH DRAKE, WELSH FALCONER, WELSH PARROT.

**Welsh-American:** An American of Welsh descent or that which relates to Wales and America. Joseph P. Clancy in his poem 'S4C' uses the word 'Americymry' (quoted by A.T. Evans 1989:14-5). In America Welsh is taught at Indiana University and the main organisation is NWAF (National Welsh-American Foundation) or Sefydliad Cenedlaethol Cymru-America. See WELSH AMERICANA, WELSH ATHENS, WELSH INDIANS, WELSH TRACT.

**Welsh Americana:** Things pertaining to Welsh-American interest. The expression is used, for example, in Prof. Edward Hartmann's *A Classified Bibliography of Welsh Americana* (1991). cf. WELSHANA.

**Welsh 'American Buffalo':** Simon Harris speaking of his own play 'Badfinger', confesses 'A lot of critics saw it as a Welsh "American Buffalo" ' (NWR 37:77, 1997). ("American Buffalo" was a work by Mamet.)

**Welshampton:** Also Welch Hampton, a place in Shropshire. See 'WELSH NATIONAL TERRITORY'.

**Welsh Amritsar:** See WELSH DROGHEDA.

**Welshana:** Things related to Wales and Welsh interest. cf. WELSH AMERICANA.

**Welsh-Anglican:** Term used eg. by Humphreys (1983:128) to refer to 'clerical bards' eg. John Jenkins (Ifor Ceri). See WELSH

PREACHER POET. Garlick refers to them as 'Welsh Anglican parson poets' (1970:36)

**Welsh anglo-phone:** M. Wynn Thomas uses this term to refer to Anglo-Welsh literature (NWR 38:86, 1997). Yet it could also be applied to an Anglo-Welsh person.

**Welsh Annals:** 'Annales Cambriae'. 3 sets of annals ed. by John Williams 1860, the first of which was written c1100 and containing annals from 445-954.

**Welsh Antipodes:** See WELSH AUSTRALIAN, WELSH KIWI.

**Welsh Apostle:** Or the 'Apostle of Wales' an epithet for St David (see WELSH PATRON SAINT). Other 'Welsh apostles' includes: The Apostle of Carmarthenshire (Stephen Hughes 1622-88) translator of 'Pilgrim's Progress', The Apostle of Liberty (Richard Price 1723-91) minister and philosopher, The Apostle of Peace (Henry Richard 1812-88) political reformer. See also WELSH NATIONALISM, THE APOSTLE OF.

**Welsh Arcadia:** Brewer describes Arcadia as 'a byword for rustic bliss'. Humphreys writes of the period 1588-1789:

'This was the essence of the Pax Anglicana and as prosperity slowly returned after the wars it continued as a background noise, like the hum of bees and insects in the quiet glades of the Welsh Arcadia' (1983:73).

**Welsh arch:** Small flat arch built into masonry (also called a jack arch). The arch is over a space of 300mm. above a stretcher and two identical corbelled pillars. See WELSH GROIN, WELSH VAULT.

**Welsh-arched:** With a WELSH ARCH.

**'Welsh Argentinean':** A WELSH SETTLER of Patagonia who has become Argentine in his custom. Glyn Williams describes what is 'referred to as the 'Welsh Argentinean' . . . This was the young man who spurned the settled life, choosing instead to roam the interior on horseback, the 'gaucho' his model of behaviour . . . ' (1991:125)

**Welsh archers:** See WELSH BOWMEN.

**Welsh arching:** The making of a WELSH ARCH (qv.).

**Welsh-Argentine:** See WELSH PATAGONIANS, WELSH-TEHUELCHE. Some writers use the form Argentine-Welsh (eg. Ellis 1985:177).

**Welsh-Armoric:** Pertaining to both Wales and Brittany (Armorica). See WELSH-BRETON SWORD.

**Welsh Arms:** No relation to 'Irish Arms' (which refers to thick legs). See WELSH COAT OF ARMS.

**'Welsh Arrangers':** (Y Trefnyddion Cymraeg) : See The WELSH ORGANISERS.

**Welsh-Arthurian:** (Peyton 1996:74): That which pertains to the Welsh Arthurian tradition.

**Welsh A School:** See WELSH CATEGORY A SCHOOL.

**Welsh A Section:** See WELSH PONY SECTION A.

**Welsh Assembly:** See WELSH PARLIAMENT.

**Welsh Association:** May writes that in 1742 'The first Welsh Association (Sasiwn) of Methodists was held at Deugoedydd near Llandovery' (1994:95). See WELSH METHODISTS.

**Welsh Athens (of America), The:** So the large Welsh community of Scranton, Pennsylvania was dubbed (see Petro 1994: 107-8). Similarly the Athens of the North was Edinburgh (also called the Modern Athens), the Athens of Ireland – Belfast, the Athens of the New World – Boston, the Athens of the West – Cordoba in the middle ages. Lecce is 'The Athens of Puglia', S. Italy ('Odyssey', Vol.2, No.2, p.38, 1994). See also The WELSH STRIKE. cf. WELSH BARCELONA, WELSH BIARRITZ, WELSH BLACKPOOL, WELSH CHICAGO etc.

**Welsh Atlantis:** Cantre'r Gwaelod, submerged land of Gwyddno Garanhir. The land (lying under the Cardigan Bay) was flooded when the well-maiden Mererid (or in another version Seithenyn) let the water through the dyke. Off Cornwall, the 'Cornish Atlantis' was the land of Lyonesse joining Cornwall to the Scilly Isles. In Breton folklore, the land of Ker Ys was also drowned. More recently there has been the drowning of Cwm Tryweryn – similar to Richard Burton's film debut 'The Last Days of Dolwyn' (1948) about a Welsh valley village drowned to make a reservoir. A reference to the 'Welsh Atlantis' is in Colfey (1981:53). See WELSH EDEN, WELSH ELDORADO, WELSH SODOM, WELSH XANADU.

**Welsh at-risk list:** Clive Betts writes that Capel y Cymmer, oldest chapel in Rhondda 'has been placed at the top of the Welsh at-risk list by the chairman of a Government heritage quango' (Western Mail, Wed. Dec. 28th, 1994).

**Welsh auction:** In contrast with a standard auction (where price is raised) or a Dutch auction (where it is reduced in bargaining) in a Welsh auction the trader adds an item/items (or to quantity) until the customer agrees to buy without actually changing the price. English speakers of the border region use this phrase and apparently this mode of sale can still be seen at some fairs/ffeiriau – especially at Machynlleth.

**Welsh Augustans:** Glyn Jones refers to this as an accepted 'literary term' (Planet 112: 72, August/September 1995). In 1924 Saunders Lewis published *A School of Welsh Augustans*. The name is analogous with the neo-classical literary period of Defoe, Pope Swift et al. (which in term took its name from the period of Augustus (and works of Virgil, Horace and Livy). See WELSH HORACE, WELSH VIRGIL.

**Welsh aunt:** See WELSH COUSIN, WELSH UNCLE.

**Welsh auntie:** 'Bopa', John Edwards' form of WELSH AUNT (1985:13).

**Welsh-Australian:** 1) A 'Wozzie' or Welsh person settled in Australia (not to be confused with a Waler/sometimes called Welsher – a horse from New South Wales). 2) Also that which relates to both Wales and Australia. See WELSH BOOMERANG, WELSHER.

**Welsh B:** WELSH PONY SECTION B. See WELSH

MOUNTAIN PONY SECTION A, WELSH PONY OF COB TYPE SECTION C. WELSH COB SECTION D.

**Welsh Baccalaureate:** Welsh BAC (BAC Cymreig). Brainchild of Colin Jenkins and John David, intended to replace the current 'A' level systems (Planet 125:116-7, 1997).

**Welsh bacon settle:** Type of old oak settle made in Wales.

**Welsh badge:** See WELSH BADGE MOTTO.

**'Welsh badge motto':** So MacDonald (1970:44) labels the motto 'Y Ddraig Goch Ddyry Gychwyn' (The Red Dragon will show the way). These words were added to the Red Dragon badge in 1953.

**Welsh bagpipes:** (Y Got-bib). Apart from the pibgorn (see WELSH HORNPIPE) there was also a Welsh bagpipe. The piohb mhór or Great Highland Bagpipe of Scotland and the piob uillean (uilleann pipe) of Ireland are well known. Yet other Celtic nations like Wales have reasserted a bagpipe tradition. In Cornwall the 'Cornish bagpipes' are distinct and called pybaw sagh, (Cornwall even has an official Cornish piper). In Brittany there is the biniou and in the Isle of Mann the poibberaght. See Woodhouse (1994:25). See WELSH CROWD, WELSH DOUBLE HORNPIPE, WELSH FIDDLE, WELSH HARP, WELSH VIOLIN.

**Welsh bait:** (Ox.) A rest on top of a hill but without refreshment. cf. Irishman's rest – going up a friend's ladder with a hod of bricks and a Scotch bait – halt and rest on one's staff as practised by pedlars (also DHS).

**Welsh-baked:** Baked in Wales or in Welsh style.

**'Welsh bakestone breads':** A category of Welsh breads made in bakestone style. Freeman uses the term (1996:27).

**Welsh bakestones:** (Bara maen, bara llech faen, bara planc). Sweet bread placed on griddle stone. See WELSH CAKES.

**'Welsh Balor':** Yspaddaden Pencawr. The giant whose daughter's marriage to Culhwch seals his fate. Matthews and

Matthews therefore refer to him as 'the Welsh counterpart of Balor' (1988:167). Likewise in Irish mythology, Balor was to be killed by his own grandson according to prophecy. Hence both Balor and Yspaddaden tried to prevent their daughters (Ethlinn and Olwen respectively) from marrying.

**Welsh 'Band Aid' Song:** In the Sain album 'Swynol Sain' 1985. (See Sain 1997-1998 Catalogue, p.72).

**'Welsh bandy':** As Iain C. Uallas calls 'bando' or WELSH HOCKEY (qv.) (Carn No.97, Spring 1997, p.13), to distinguish it from English and other Celtic variations.

**Welsh Bangor:** As opposed to the Bangor in Co. Down, N. Ireland.

**Welsh bank-notes:** In Patagonia in the WELSH COLONY/WELSH SETTLEMENT (qv.) 'Welsh bank-notes were printed' (Stephens ed. 1986:464). Sikes tells us that Welsh fairies also used money (1880:119). See WELSH PASSPORT, WELSH POUND, WELSH STAMPS.

**Welsh banner:** See WELSH FLAG.

**'Welsh Banshee':** Rhys (1901:452-3), Briggs (1976:210) and Matthews and Matthews (1988:89) refer to the 'Gwrach y Rhibyn' or 'Hag of Warning' as the 'Welsh Banshee'. She is an apparition with a terrible scream and warns of death. See also 'WELSH WASHER OF THE FORD'.

**Welsh Barcelona:** Reference to Huw Thomas' review of *Cardiff: Half-and-Half a Capital* by Rhodri Morgan. Thomas describes 'Rhodri Morgan's vision of Cardiff as a kind of Barcelona (to London's Madrid)' (Planet 109:104. Feb/March 1995). cf. WELSH ATHENS, WELSH BIARRITZ, WELSH BLACKPOOL, WELSH CAPITAL, WELSH CHICAGO, WELSH 'GAY CAPITAL'.

**Welsh Bard:** Morris says of Lloyd George: 'It was above all as a Welshman that he was always known in England – 'The WELSH WIZARD', 'The Welsh Bard', 'The Merlin of Politics' . . . ' (1995:10).

**Welsh bardic name** (enw barddol): Poet's name once he has been initiated into Gorsedd.

**Welsh Bards, Society of:** As Villiers calls the Gorsedd (1965:730).

**'Welsh barley sheaf'** (Geifr): A sheaf which is tied upwards. For illustration see Lady Llanover (1867:257, plate 6).
cf. WELSH WHEATSTOOK.

**'Welsh Barn Dance':** The 'Dawnsie Twmpath'. See book of same name by Eddie Jones (Y Lolfa).

**Welsh Barons of Wales:** As R.R. Davies refers to the native Welsh rulers whose status was diminished after time of Edward I (Herbert & Jones eds. 1988:4).

**Welsh 'barony'** (barwniaeth Gymraeg): A Welsh area in Pennsylvania (Humphreys 1983:71). See WELSH TRACT.

**'Welsh baseball'** (pêl fâs Gymreig): Copied by Americans as baseball.

**Welsh-based:** (Of a film or company, book etc.) based on/in Wales.

**Welsh-bashing:** (Literally and metaphorically) persecution of Welsh people. cf. Paki-bashing.

**'Welsh bastion of the Silures':** As Mathias calls the S.E. of Wales, the Silures being a dark Welsh tribe (1987:70).

**Welsh BBC 1:** Really BBC Wales/Cymru. Along with HTV Cymru provided only a minimal source of Welsh T.V. programmes before the WELSH FOURTH CHANNEL (qv.).

**Welsh Beacons:** Alternative name for the preferred term 'Brecon Beacons'. ('The Welsh Beacon' is also a magazine for WELSH PONY SECTIONS A and B.)

**Welsh bean:** French/kidney bean. See WELSH NUT.

**Welsh Beauty:** A variety of apple shown at the 1892 RHS exhibition but now lost (see Smith 1971). Possibly it is to be identified with the Monmouthshire Beauty (an apple also called

'Cissy' or 'Tampling' – see Roderick 1994:112). cf. WELSH PIPPIN, WELSH'S SPITZENBERG.

**Welsh beaver hat** (het befar gymreig): See WELSH HAT.

**Welsh bedding:** Sleeping together before/outside marriage (see ap Huw 1995:11). This seems distinct from 'bundling' or 'caru ar/yn y gwely' or 'love on/in the bed' (see Stevens 1993:82-94, 97-112) which may not always have been sexual. Hazlitt describes 'bundling' as 'a widely diffused Welsh custom before marriage' (1905:81) yet it was universal – in parts of England, Holland and even existed as 'yobai' in Japan (see Kerr 1993:269). So why should Welsh people be singled out for this! See also WELSH WIFE (qv.).

**Welsh Beef Stew:** A recipe of beef, potatoes, carrots, onion, swede and bacon (see Grant 1993:19).

**Welsh beetle** (chrysolina cerealis): A beautiful beetle found only in a small area of Snowdon. cf. WELSHMAN'S BUTTON, WELSH CLEAR-WING, WELSH WAVE.

**Welsh-begotten:** See WELSH-BORN.

**Welsh-belted:** Really it should be belted Welsh (Bolian Cymru), a breed of Welsh sheep. See WELSH MOUNTAIN.

**Welsh bet:** See WELSH A BET, WELSHER.

**Welsh Biarritz:** Aberystwyth. The epithet derives from an 1860's advertisement billing Aberystwyth as 'The Biarritz of the Cambrian Coast'. See WELSH BLACKPOOL, WELSH GAY CAPITAL, WELSH NAPLES, WELSH RIVIERA.

**Welsh Bible Box:** M.E. Jones writes 'A mule chest had two small drawers beneath it. Known as "y coffer bach" and the Welsh Bible Box, it is a type of its own' (1978:68). It was made of oak, elm or holly for inlaid work, the Bible was kept within and family papers inside the small drawer below.

**Welsh Bicknor:** In Heref. & Worcs., so called 'from its situation on the Welsh side of the River Wye' (Mills, 1996:34;351). cf. WELSH FRANKTON.

**Welsh bill:** A weapon – bill-hook. See WELSH GLAIVE, WELSH HOOK.

**Welsh bill-hook:** See WELSH BILL.

**'Welsh Bill of Rights':** Phrase used to refer to what Welsh activists demand (The Welsh Monitor, Vol.8, No.5, Sept./Oct. 1995).

**Welsh Birmingham:** Palfrey and Roberts write about Llanfair P.G., 'certain cynical Welsh patriots have translated this very long place name as "Birmingham-by-the-sea" ' (1994:54).

**Welsh Black** ([Gwartheg] Duon Cymreig): A famous dual purpose breed of cattle (ie. used both for dairy produce and beef) native to Wales. See WELSH BULL, WELSH RUNT, WELSH-SPEAKING COW.

**Welsh Black beef burger:** Safer than non-Welsh beefburger with mad cow disease ('Western Mail: Country and Farming', Tues. 23 September, 1997, p.3).

**Welsh Black Cattle:** See WELSH BLACK.

**Welsh Black Cattle Society** (Cymdeithas Gwartheg Duon Cymreig): f.1904.

**Welsh black-pointed breed:** A representative of an old breed. A white Welsh breed with black points derived from white specimens born of black Welsh cows.

**Welsh Blackpool:** 1) 'Rhyl – also called the WELSH MARGATE (qv.). 2) Perhaps Porthcawl would also be a suitable candidate for this appellation. Palfrey and Roberts describe Porthcawl as 'The closest thing to a Welsh equivalent of Blackpool' (1994:71). cf. WELSH MARGATE, WELSH RIVIERA. See WELSH BIARRITZ, WELSH RIVIERA.

**Welsh Blacks:** 1) WELSH BLACK cattle (qv.) 2) See also WELSH NIGGERS.

**'Welsh black oats'** (ceirch-du-bach): An old variety of native Welsh oats (see W. Meredith Morris 1910:67).

**'Welsh blankets':** Coarse blankets of WELSH WOOL, as

opposed to the Witney blanket of Lowland wool (A.M. Jones 1927:32).

**Welsh Blockheads:** Also 'Whish Blockheads'. Standard shout for those who did poorly in spelling tests, especially when the tests were done as team games (see Parry-Jones 1964:157). cf. WELSH NOT. See WELSH HEADS.

**'Welsh bloodlines':** Term referring to the pedigree of WELSH PONIES and WELSH COBS.

**'Welsh blood, Registered':** Phrase the WELSH PONY AND COB SOCIETY uses in reference to the not less than 25% pedigree of the so-called WELSH PART BRED (qv.).

**Welsh Bluebeard:** Robert Vaughan (not to be confused with the anti-quarian of same name). Despite his epithet he did not murder his wives but innocent souls whose ships he lured with lights on sheep near his home in Dunraven castle. The Cornish Bluebeard is the ogre Tregeagle.

**Welsh blue stones:** The stones forming the inner circle of Stonehenge. In 1922 Welsh geologist H.H. Jones proved that their unique composition of 'spotted dolerite' meant that they were from Prescelly.

**Welsh boers:** See WELSH BOORS.

**'Welsh Bomber':** John Jenkins (so he is billed in advertisement for his 'Prison Letters'). See WELSH SUMMER HOUSES.

**Welsh bonnet:** The Welsh bonnet had frills smoothed by a special heater called a 'talian'. See WELSH CAP, WELSH HAT, WELSH WIG.

**Welsh Book of the Year** (Llyfr y Flwyddyn): Book voted the best in Wales each year.

**Welsh boomerang:** 'We'll take time out to meet Dai Evans, inventor of the Welsh boomerang. It doesn't come back, it just sings about coming back' (by the Two Ronnies, quoted in McArthur (ed.) 1992:381). See WELSH JOKE.

**Welsh Boors:** A triple pun by Jane Aaron: 'The order of society is that the Welsh boors will of course be subordinate in their own country to English ladies and gentlemen. Wild boars can be dangerous, however' (NWR 27:36, Winter 1994-95).

**Welsh Boot Hill:** Alluding to the western frontier cemetry Glyn Jones writes with reference to Anglo-Welsh literature that 'it is unlikely that editions of the present editors will be buried in a Welsh Boot Hill.' (1971:pxvi). By contrast, The Scottish Boot Hill is near Scone where the kings were crowned (see Guthrie 1885:105).

**'Welsh boot-lickers':** See 'WELSH LICKSPITTLES'.

**Welsh Border:** The Region on the borders of England and Wales. The old border was Offa's Dyke C8th from Prestatyn to Sedbury built by Offa King of Mercia. See WELSH MARCHES.

**Welsh Border Country:** See WELSH BORDER.

**Welsh Borderers:** People from the WELSH BORDER (qv.).

**Welsh Borderland:** See WELSH BORDER.

**Welsh Borderlands:** See WELSH BORDER.

**Welsh border fan:** This type of corn dolly is still made by Christina's Crafts, St Austell. See WELSH FAN, WELSH HAG.

**Welsh Border Morris:** A particular variety of Morris dancing. Hutton writes 'Today this tradition is called "Welsh Border Morris", another partial misnomer as it was rarest near the border itself'. It was performed at Christmas with blackened faces and 'instead of ribbons, gaudy rags were usually employed to decorated shirts' (1996:269).

**'Welsh Border Tart':** A recipe with shortcrust pastry, sultanas, raisins and cinnamon (Smeeth 1994:42). No relation to WELSH WIFE.

**Welsh-born:** Born in Wales; or born of Welsh parents.

**Welsh bowmen:** Instrumental in victory at Agincourt (1415). Even today The Society of The Black Hundred (descendants of bowmen of Crécy and Poitiers) have annual ceremony in Llantrisant. They may also have been the 'group of phantom bowmen firing their flights of silvery arrows into the advancing German troops' in WW1 shortly after Welsh poet's prophetic *The Bowmen* was published (see Haining 1982:19-21). See WELSH LONG BOW.

**Welsh box-bed** (Y Gwely Bocs): A bed built in a cupboard (see NWR 21:19). In Dyfed it was called 'gwely-cwpwrd' (Morris 1910). It is similar to the Breton 'lit clos', the Irish 'settle bed' (Joyce) and the Cornish 'cupboard bed' (O.C. Vol.X. No.3 1986:120).

**Welshboy:** (One word). cf. WELSHMAN, WELSHWOMAN.

**Welshboyo:** (One or two words). cf. WELSHO.

**Welsh Braveheart:** Dewi Roberts writes 'The splendid film "Braveheart" presented the tumultuous life of William Wallace in an unforgettable way. Let us hope that a film of equal quality is made taking Glyndŵr as its subject . . . ' (BWA 48, July '97, p.8). Similarly Payton describes Michael Joseph (An Gof – The Smith) as 'The Cornish Braveheart' (1996:125).

**'Welsh Bread':** 1) Bara Cymraeg – with white and brown flour, yeast, sugar, butter, salt and water (Smith-Twiddy 1979:19). 2) So Bogle calls 'bara brith' (1988:85). See WELSH CURRANT BREAD.

**Welsh bread and cheese cupboard:** A unique piece of Welsh furniture like the 'cwpwrdd-deuddarn' (two-part cupboard) but smaller. cf. WELSH DRESSER.

**'Welsh Bread Pudding':** A recipe utilising left over/stale bread, sultanas, raisins, currants, flour, sugar, milk, grated apple and margarine (see Grant 1993:58).

**'Welsh breakfast':** 1) A good cooked breakfast consisting of laverbread (see WELSH CAVIARE) etc. (Smeeth 1994:8). 2) On the lines of English Breakfast, Welsh Breakfast (like WELSH AFTERNOON) is a distinct blend of tea by Gwynedd Confectioners.

**'Welsh bred Hereford cattle':** 'Famous throughout the world are the Welsh bred Hereford cattle' (Miles 1969:188). cf. WELSH

21

BLACKS.

**'Welsh breeds'** (bridiau Cymreig): See WELSH BLACK, WELSH COB, WELSH MOUNTAIN, WELSH PONY etc.

**Welsh-Breton Sword** (Cleddyf Deuddarn): A Split sword – gift from Brittany to Wales in 1899, symbolising their union (the Welsh half has designs of WELSH LEEK and WELSH DRAGON and the Breton half shows the arms of Duchess Anne).

**'Welsh Bridge':** 1) Not the game of bridge at all but a simple card game probably the same as 'elevens', in which player on his own lays out nine cards covering pairs eg. 5 and 6 which make eleven. 2) The 'Welsh Bridge' was passed to enter Shrewsbury as opposed to the 'English Bridge' over the Severn (Piehler 1935:147).

**Welsh brief:** (Ox.) meaning now obscure.

**Welsh Brigade:** Miles, with reference to the reductions in the Welsh Regiments, writes 'when the pruning is finished only the WELSH GUARDS and two regular battalions forming the WELSH BRIGADE will remain' (1969:185).

**'Welsh British':** See WELSH GLOBAL.

**Welsh Briton:** A famous WELSH PONY (see Davies 1993:8).

**Welsh Broth** (Cawl Cymru): 1) A broth of WELSH LAMB, carrots, turnips, onion, barley, mixed herbs, salt and pepper (Sian Llewellyn 1974:49). cf. WELSH CAWL. 'Welsh broth' also means treachery. cf. Ger. Welsches Süpplein (J. Green 1996:295). See WELSH FAITH.

**Welsh Brownie:** So Briggs calls the 'Bwca' and 'Bwbachod' (1976:55-6). See WELSH CHANGELING, WELSH HOUSE-HOLD SPIRIT.

**'Welsh Brython':** A Briton of Wales, as opposed to one from Cornwall or Brittany. G. Evans uses the term (1974:77).

**Welsh B School:** See WELSH CATEGORY A SCHOOL.

**Welsh Buccaneer:** Henry Morgan (d.1688). Barti Ddu and

Tomos Prys were other pirates.

**Welsh buffooneries:** (In reference to Dylan Thomas-type plays) 'By about 1950 – the market in England for Welsh buffooneries was disappearing' (Stephens, ed. 1986:551). cf. WELSH PAGLIACCI.

**Welsh bugle-leafed speedwell:** See WELSH SPEEDWELL.

**Welsh-built:** Built in Wales, in Welsh style, by Welsh people, eg. WELSH D-SHAPED CASTLE.

**Welsh Bull, Black:** The Tristan Da Cunha series of 'Island Animals' stamps (26.8.97) features Border Collies, Black Face Rams, Black Welsh Bull and Chickens. cf. WELSH STAMPS.

**'Welsh Buns':** Buns made with butter, castor sugar and eggs (Smeeth 1994:33). cf. WELSH CAKES.

**Welsh Bunyan:** Also The Bunyan of Wales (Azariah Shadrach 1774-1844). The Cornish Bunyan is Jack Clemo (see Cornwall Today, No.3, Sept. 1994, p.21).

**Welshburg:** Also Welchburg, a place name.

**Welsh Burns:** Piehler, in reference to Llanfair Talhaiarn says it is the place 'where "Talhaiarn", the Welsh Burns (John Jones, d.1869), is buried' (1935:215).

**Welsh Bus, Old Model:** One of the Corgi (qv. WELSH CORGI) Classics with a red roof, WELSH DRAGON and 'Cymru am Byth'.

**Welsh Business Bible** (Y Beibl Busnes Cymraeg): So Menter a Busnes is called (Contact Bulletin, Vol.9. 1. Spring 1992:7).

**'Welsh butter':** A salty type of butter used in many Welsh recipes.

**Welsh butter toffee:** Another term for WELSH TOFFEE (qv.). (Freeman 1996:244).

**'Welsh by choice':** N. Jones' category of a WELSHPERSON, referring to someone who has chosen to be Welsh (especially if non-Welsh) (1993:30 and 162). cf. WELSH CONVERT.

**Welsh Byegones:** Old Welsh folk items. Peate writes 'There was in the Department of Archeology in the National Museum of Wales, a small but representative collection of what were called 'Welsh Byegones' (1972:17)'.

**'Welsh by proxy':** Caldwell uses this term similarly to WELSH-ADOPTED (Bowie & Davies eds. 1992:157,161).

**'Welsh by self-election':** A category of Welshman who is Welsh by choice not birth or blood. Horvie, refers to novelist Richard Hughes as 'Welsh by self-election rather than origin' (Herbert & Jones eds. 1995:160).

**Welsh C:** See WELSH PONY SECTION A.

**'Welsh Caerphilly':** To distinguish it from non-Welsh imitations, Smeeth feels that the 'Welsh' is essential (1994:109). It is indispensable for WELSH TOASTED CHEESE (qv.)

**Welsh Caesar Augustus:** In reference to the emperor who at death commanded that his empire not be extended, Humphreys writes cynically about Lloyd George that:
'The census held in the penultimate year of the Welsh Caesar Augustus, 1921, revealed that the percentage of his mother tongue in his native country had sunk to thirty-seven' (1983:209). See WELSHMAN, THE LITTLE and WELSH WIZARD.

**Welsh Cajun:** Louisiana-style Welsh country music eg. the album 'Cajuns Denbo: Stompio' (Sain).

**Welshcakes:** (Can be spelt as one word). See WELSH CAKES.

**Welsh cakes** (Picau/pice ar y maen, teisennau cri): bakestones cooked on a griddle.

**Welsh cakes, sweet:** A WELSH CAKE recipe with more sugar and nutmeg (1994:40).

**Welsh Calvinistic Methodists:** See WELSH PRESBYTERIANS.

**Welsh Calvinistic Methodist Mission:** WELSH PRESBYTERIAN mission abroad, especially in N.E. India. qv. Nigel Jenkins' 'Gwalia in Khasia' (Gomer).

**Welsh Calvinistic Mystics:** See D. Ben Rees' review of R.M. Jones' 'Cyfriniaeth Gymraeg' (NWR 28:97, Spring 1995).

**Welsh Cambria:** A tautology (see Humphreys 1983:136) since Cambria means Wales.

**Welsh-Cambrian:** Another tautology found for example in The Welsh Cambrian Society, Christchurch, New Zealand.

**Welsh Camp:** Nickname for the field between Lamb's Conduit and Gray's Inn Lane, London, C17th-C18th.

**Welsh Campaign** (1294): Edward's military campaign against the Welsh.

**Welsh Campaign for Civil and Political Liberties:** Formed after activists, including members of the WELSH SOCIALIST REPUBLICAN MOVEMENT were arrested in police raids eg. Operation Fire in April 1980 for alleged burning of WELSH SUMMER HOUSES etc. See WELSH POLITICAL PRISONERS' DEFENCE COMMITTEE.

**Welsh Canal Act:** The First, passed in 1766 for a canal from Kidwelly to Carway, Gwendraeth Fawr Valley (May 1994:141).

**'Welsh candle snuffers':** Seen at Jerusalem and Bethesda Presbyterian Churches booth in the 1997 Welsh National Gymanfa Ganu, Milwaukee.

**Welsh Canterbury:** As Llandaff has been called. Or 'The Canterbury of Wales'.

**Welsh cap:** Highest award for Welsh rugby; also for football eg. Fred Keenor (d.1972) captain of Cardiff City/Bluebirds 'won thirty-two Welsh caps' (Stephens ed. 1986:332). cf. WELSH HAT.

**Welsh Capital:** Since 1955 Cardiff (Caerdydd). In trucker's language it is called Daffodil Capital (Moore 1981:32) (see WELSH DAFFODIL). Rhodri Morgan calls Cardiff 'Half and Half a Capital' (Gomer 1994). Swansea is often referred to as Wales' Second Capital. Aberystwyth is the 'Capital of Mid Wales' (Thomas 1990:41). Liverpool is the Capital of North

Wales. Moreover, Trosset argues that for many Welsh people 'The capital of Wales each year was where the National Eisteddfod was held' (1993:20). Also Merthyr Tydfil was once called 'Iron Capital of the World' (quoted in 'Valley Breaks '97' brochure). See WELSH BARCELONA, WELSH CHICAGO, WELSH GAY CAPITAL, WELSH METROPOLIS, WELSH QUARTER.

**Welsh capping:** Game of giving a Welsh word and its translation and vice versa and then giving the opposite meaning (Parry-Jones 1964:160).

**'Welsh Captain', The:** 1) Shakespeare's Fluellen (Llewelyn?). Perhaps the original Fluellen was Davy Gam who saved Henry V's life at Agincourt. See WELSH BOWMEN. 2) The Captain of the Welsh rugby team (see Humphreys & Bennet). cf. WELSH CAP.

**Welsh Cardigan(shire) Corgi:** Also Cardigan Welsh Corgi (Corgi Ceredigion). See WELSH CORGI, WELSH DORGI.

**Welsh Carol Singing:** So Llewellyn calls the 'Plygain' (1974:5) or early morning carol service on Christmas Day in the Tanad Valley. Similar services are The Manx Oei'l Verney, the Norwegian julotte, the Breton Oferennar Pelgent and Catalan miss del gall (the last two, like 'plygain' related to the word 'cock' in reference to the early hour of the cock's crow).

**Welsh carpet:** Unlike a Scotch carpet (one made in Kidderminster), the Welsh carpet is patterned bricks and dockleaf juice (ox.). Indeed, rather than a joke this may have been true. Baker refers to 'The Welsh liking for Sycamore leaves as a stencil for whitened kitchen floors' (1996:147). cf. WELSH LAY, WELSH LUMP, WELSH RAG, WELSH TAPESTRY.

**Welsh carrot plum pudding:** Recipe of Lady Llanover (1867:457) with raisins, currants, suet, lemon peel, nutmeg, carrots and flour.

**Welsh cart-horse:** Perhaps once a distinct breed. Vaughan-Thomas says of the WELSH COB (qv.) that 'some insist that it springs from an animal vaguely described as 'the old Welsh cart-horse'.' (1981:193). In the laws of Hywel Dda one of the three types of Welsh horses mentioned was equus operarins (working horse) who could pull a gambo or sledge (the others were palfrey – riding pony and rowney/sumper – packhorse).

**'Welsh cat':** Also called 'Cymric' (in Canada) or 'long-haired Manx', is a breed like the Manx-cat which is tailless. Maybe there is some confusion with the 'ci Môn' o'r 'Anglesey dog' without a tail mentioned by Gerald of Wales (could Môn have been confused with Manaw – Isle of Man?). (There is a tailless breed of dog called schippenke or Du. 'little boatmen' – a watch dog on barges).

**Welsh Category A School:** School in which the WELSH LANGUAGE is the main language, all subjects being taught through the medium of Welsh. Category A caters for pupils mainly in the WELSH HEARTLAND, category B catering for a mixed area and providing more English-medium education. Category C is for a Welsh School in a WELSHLESS area where all the curriculum is English-based.

**Welsh Catholic Martyrs:** C16th and C17th martyrs – Philip Evans, Richard Gwyn, John Jones, David Lewis, John Lloyd and John Roberts canonised on Oct. 25th 1970 by Pope Paul VI. Interestingly in 1987, at the beatification ceremony of three Welsh Catholic martyrs, Welsh was used in the Vatican for the first time.

**Welsh Cattle:** No relation to the Scotch Cattle (Welsh activist workers 1920-35), see WELSH BLACK.

**Welsh Cattle Drovers:** As some writers eg. Richard J. Colyer (from his book title) refer to the WELSH DROVERS (qv.).

**Welsh 'caudillos':** Leaders of the WELSH COLONY. In relation to their WELSH LANGUAGE, Argentine newspapers wrote: 'Those Welsh caudillos carry out propaganda in opposition to assimilation and obedience, stirring up conflicts with the Territorial authorities . . . ' (El Caudillo was the epithet of

Franco). (Quoted and trans. by G. Williams 1991:243) cf.

**Welsh Cavalry Regiment:** The 1st Queens Dragoon Guards (see Moreton IGW 1989:138). See WELSH FUSILIERS, WELSH GUARDS, WELSH REGIMENT.

**'Welsh cave legends':** How Rhys designates the WELSH CAVETALE (1901:456).

**'Welsh cavetale':** A category of Welsh legend mentioned by Roberts (1985:59) referring particularly to the ogofeydd Arthur (caves of Arthur) where the hero king is supposed to be sleeping.

**Welsh caviar:** See WELSH CAVIARE.

**Welsh caviare** (bara lawr, llafan, menyn y môr): The edible seaweed porphyra umbilicalis which is cooked as a welsh speciality.

**'Welsh cawl':** Broth of lambstock, parsnip, swede, turnips, carrots, celery, leeks, potatoes and herbs (Smeeth 1994:49). cf. WELSH BROTH, WELSH SOUP.

**Welsh Celtic Round-house:** How the WELSH ROUND HOUSE (qv.) is called in *Leisure Line Magazine'* (September 1991 p.6).

**Welsh Celtic Weekend:** Organised by the Slate Belt Welsh Society (see *The Eagle and The Dragon,* Vol.X, No.3, July 1996, p.6).

**Welsh-centred:** Centred on Wales or the Welsh people or language.

**'Welsh chafer':** (Hoplia philanthus) the laver of which is a problem to the roots of plants (Kindersley 1992:572).

**'Welsh Champion',** The: Newport boxer William Charles (fl.1830s) who fought on 'Bloody Field' near Thomas Street (Roderick 1994:154).

**'Welsh Changeling':** Thus Briggs calls the plentyn newydd or 'new child' (changed by the tylwyth teg or fairies for a real child) (1976:332). In Wales the changeling child is also known as 'crimbil'. See WELSH BANSHEE, WELSH BROWNIE.

**Welsh Channel:** See WELSH FOURTH CHANNEL.

**Welsh Channel Four:** See WELSH FOURTH CHANNEL.

**Welsh Champion, Royal:** Winning specimen of WELSH SHEEP breeds or WELSH PONY and WELSH COB sections in the Royal WELSH AGRICULTURAL SHOW, ROYAL.

**Welsh char:** Or Llanberris char or red-bellied char (salmonidae: salvelinus alpinus perissi – in Welsh 'torgoch') which is peculiar to Wales. The gwyniad in Bala Lake is also unique to Wales. See WELSH SEA TROUT.

**Welsh charity school:** See WELSH CIRCULATING SCHOOL.

**Welsh Charity-school:** Hyphenated form of WELSH CHARITY SCHOOL (Jones and Davies 1986:53, 103).

**Welsh Chartists:** Followers of John Frost et al. who believed in a People's Charter with 6 points (male suffrage, secret ballot, no property qualification for Mps, payment of Mps, equal constituencies, annual parliaments) which culminated in the bloody suppression at the Westgate, Newport, Nov. 1839. The word 'Welsh' is often prefixed to the chartists in Wales since 'Welsh Chartists', as distinct from their English counterparts, were anti-Anglican Church (Searby 1986:19): moreover, 'Welsh Chartists' were known for their 'anti-English sentiments' (G. Evans: 1988:216) and most were Welsh-speaking.

**'Welsh chattering class':** Kevin Williams, with reference to the progress of Cardiff says 'The Welsh chattering class . . . is part of the problem' (Planet 121:9).

**Welsh Checkpoint Charlie:** Tom Davies begins his article on Tiger Bay as follows: 'Stand under the railway bridge at the north end of Bute Street and you will know what it is like to be at a Welsh Checkpoint Charlie' (NWR 15:16, winter 1991/92). See WELSH SOHO.

**Welsh Cheddar:** An imitation of Cheddar made in Wales. cf. Scottish Cheddar. See WELSH CHEESE.

**Welsh cheese:** A name for Caerphilly cheese. In Welsh it is called 'caws Cymru' (Tibbott 1983:82). Grant 'pleonastically' prefixes the word 'welsh' calling it 'Welsh Caerphilly cheese' (1993:62), perhaps to distinguish it from non-Welsh imitations. See WELSH CHEDDAR.

**'Welsh Cheese Bake':** A recipe with sliced leeks, slices of bread, low fat spread, eggs, cheddar cheese and skimmed milk (found in The Flour Advisory Bureau's leaflet 'Six is Good for You').

**'Welsh Cheese Cake':** A unique Welsh variation of cheese cake made with Caerphilly cheese and egg yolk etc. (Freeman 1996:182).

**'Welsh Cheese Pudding'** (Pwdin Caws Pobi Cymreig): Dish of bread without crusts, cheddar, butter, egg, milk, dry mustard, cayenne pepper, nutmeg baked in oven (Freeman 1996:157).

**Welsh chess:** The ancient boardgame of 'gwyddbwyll' (not to be confused with the board game 'fox and geese') – the etymology is not gŵydd-goose but gwŷdd-trees and corresponds with the Irish 'fidchell' or 'wooden wisdom'. A similar game in Ireland was brandubh (its meaning in Welsh would be brân ddu). Hazlitt describes chess proper as 'a British or Welsh game' (1905:110). The game is mentioned in The Mabinogion and Gwenddolau ap Ceidiog's 'gwyddbwyll' (one of 13 Treasures of Britain) played by itself when the pieces were set.

**Welsh Chicago:** John Wilson calls C19th Cardiff 'The Chicago of Wales' (Planet:115:14-25, Feb./March 1996). See WELSH BARCELONA, WELSH CAPITAL.

**'Welsh chicken'** (ffowlyn Cymreig): Spring dish of chicken, bacon, carrots, leeks and cabbage (see Freeman 1988:11, Grant 1993:14).

**'Welsh Chicken Hotpot':** Hot pot of chicken, leeks, Pembroke potatoes, cider and rosemary (Grant 1993:15).

**'Welsh Chicken Pie':** A Christmas Day pie made with ham, leek and boiled chicken (M. Williams 1992:36). See WELSH COCKLE PIE.

**Welshchild:** Can be spelt as one word.

**Welsh Children's Festival** (Gŵyl Plant Cymru): A children's dancing festival organised by the WELSH FOLK DANCE SOCIETY.

**Welsh chimney pot hat:** (Cwcwll tal or hat-gopa-dal, Morris 1910:161). See WELSH HAT.

**'Welsh China'** (llestri Cymreig): The term mainly applies to early C19th Nantgarw and Swansea china.

**'Welsh Christians', 'Mecca for':** G. Evans describes Griffith Jones' parish of Llanddowror as 'a Mecca for Welsh Christians' (1988:171). See WELSH CIRCULATING SCHOOL. cf. Llangeithio which G. Evans calls 'The Mecca of Methodists' (1988:184) ie. WELSH CALVINISTIC METHODISTS.

**'Welsh Christmas-tide carols':** So 'Carolau Plygain' are called in Acen 1995-1997 Catalogue. See WELSH CAROL SINGING.

**Welsh Chronicle of the Princes:** Welsh Chronicle(s).

**Welsh Church:** Or Church in Wales. A separate and distinct church that did not accept The Roman Easter until the time of Elford, bishop in N. Wales 768. Owain Glyndŵr in his letter to the French King Charles VI declared the hope for an Independent Welsh Church free from Canterbury. See WELSH PRESBYTERIANS.

**Welsh Church Acts:** (1914 and 1919).

**Welsh Church Acts Fund:**

**Welsh Church Commission** (1906):

**Welsh Church Disestablishment:** The Disestablishment of the Church in Wales in 1920.

**Welsh Cincinnatus:** In reference to the Roman consul who in C5thBC 'returned to his plough', Mr Edwards who came to live in Ramsey said that 'like a Welsh Cincinnatus, I have retired to my farm, happy to till the land and speak with the birds and seals' (quoted by Vaughan-Thomas 1981:90).

**'Welsh Cinnamon Cake'** (Teisen Sinamon): Shallow cake of egg yolks, cinnamon, jam and meringue on top (Freeman 1996:210-1).

**Welsh circular house:** Peate's phrase (1972:25) for medieval houses. See WELSH ROUND HOUSE.

**Welsh Circulating Charity Schools** (Encycl. Brit.): See WELSH CIRCULATING SCHOOLS.

**Welsh Circulating Schools:** Schools set up by Griffith Jones (1683-1761) rector of Llanddowror with the aim of teaching people to read the Bible. cf. WELSH CHRISTIANS, MECCA FOR, WELSH FREE SCHOOLS, WELSH TRUST.

**Welsh City of Brotherly Love:** Morgan John Rhys built Beulah 'his own Welsh City of Brotherly Love, in the Allegheny Forest', (Humphreys 1983:113). See WELSH COLONY, WELSH DIASPORA, WELSH EXILES SOCIETY.

**Welsh Civil Rights Movement:** As Cefn is sometimes called (see Planet 83:116). See the WELSH LANGUAGE CIVIL RIGHTS MOVEMENT.

**Welsh Classics:** The greatest works in Welsh literature eg. Bishop Morgan's Welsh Bible 1588 etc.

**Welsh clearwing** (conopia scoliaeformis): Clearwing with clay red tuff at bottom unlike other clearwings and orange or yellow colouring with slight hornet appearance. Now believed to be extinct but so called as first specimen was found in Wales. See WELSH WAVE.

**'Welsh clog blocks':** Blocks made by the 'clociwr' and bought by factories, usually of sycamore and heavier than the Lancashire beech clog blocks (A.M. Jones, 1927:51).

**Welsh Clog Dance:** A distinct type of clog dance in Wales (mentioned in Wales Tourist Board brochure on 'hwyrnos'. qv. WELSH NIGHT). See also WELSH JIG, WELSH REEL.

**Welsh Closing Act** (1881): See WELSH SUNDAY CLOSING ACT.

**Welsh cloth:** 'Welsh cloth is referred to by many names: pannus wallie, frieze, kersey, wadmoll and brecknock' (Sutton 1987:15). See WELSH COTTON, WELSH FLANNEL, WELSH LINING, WELSH SHEEP, WELSH WOOL.

**Welsh Clover Honey:** According to Howells the best type for the WELSH LAMB, HONEY (qv.) recipe (p.16).

**Welsh clubmoss** (pilularia annotinum): See WELSH POPPY, WELSH SPEEDWELL.

**Welsh coal:** An anthricite from S. Wales, reputedly the best in the world. In 1922 sent to New York. See WELSH CULM, WELSH STONE.

**Welsh Coal Trade, Mother of the:** Lucy Thomas (1781-1847)

**Welsh Coat of Arms:** See WELSH DRAGON.

**Welsh cob** (cob Cymreig): Like the WELSH PONY (qv.) a separate breed from Wales, short-legged, strong and good to ride, can be up to 14.2 hands (a hand = 4" ). Also found in combinations like Welsh cob pony or Welsh cob filly etc. cf. WELSH CARTHORSE, WELSH KEFFEL.

**Welsh cob section D:** In competitions for WELSH PONIES and WELSH COBS, the largest division (not exceeding 13.2 hh or 137 cms). cf. WELSH PONY SECTION A.

**Welsh Cobs, The Marshland Shales of:** Epithet of famous WELSH COB Cymro Llwyd coined by Roy B. Charlton in late C19th (quoted by W. Davies 1993:62).

**Welsh Cob-type pony:** An alternative name for the WELSH PONY OF COB TYPE (qv.).

**'Welsh cockle bonnets':** Type of Welsh bonnet worn by cockle gatherers. Listed in catalog of The Harp and Dragon Craft and Gift Shop, Portland, N.Y.

**'Welsh cockle pie'** (pastai gocos): Made with cockles, bacon and spring onions. (Freeman 1996:85). See WELSH CHICKEN PIE.

**Welsh cockle plate** (plât cocos): Large beautifully decorated china plate made in Wales, especially for cockles.

**Welsh Cockney:** An incorrect term for WELSH LONDONER. Only pure Londoners (born and bred within the sound of Beau Bells) can be true Cockneys. Katie Jones also uses the term 'Cockney Welshman' (NWR.3:74, 1988).

**Welsh Codes:** The Welsh Law Codes. See WELSH LAWS.

**'Welsh coffee':** Same as 'Cornish coffee' made with honeyed mead not WELSH WHISKY; but with cream on top like Irish/Gaelic coffee. Scotch coffee, by contrast, is hot water and burnt biscuit (DHS). 'Breton coffee' or 'mic' is 'café brûlant allongé d'eau de vie de cidre' (Renouard 1992:209). Similarly, although 'Greek coffee' is a form of thick coffee also called Turkish coffee, I once saw a dreadful parody of Irish coffee called 'Greek coffee' with ouzo in. The same bar had 'Russian coffee' with vodka. Similarly there is also a 'Caribbean coffee' (with rum) (Ayto 1994:173). cf. WELSH TEA.

**Welsh coffer:** eg. Carmarthen coffer. See WELSH DRESSER etc.

**'Welsh coffin christening':** Walkley's term for the practice recorded even up to 1934 'where if a mother had died in childbirth her baby was baptized in a bowl of water on top of the coffin' (1987:17). The Welsh term is 'bedydd arch' (G.P.C., p.267).

**'Welsh Colditz':** Epithet of Island Farm Camp 128 near Bridgend for German Officer POWs. The first inmates arrived in November 1944 and on 10th March, 1945 there was a mass escape through a tunnel (Graham Smith uses the term 1993:85 and passim).

**'Welsh College':** So Jesus College, Oxford was called on account of its many Welsh students. Oriel was also called Welsh College before that (Mathias 1987:14).

**Welsh Colony,** The (Y Wladfa Gymreig): In 1856 Michael D. Jones said at speech at Bala 'in a Welsh Colony we can be imbued with a new spirit.' He sailed in The Mimosa to Argentine (see WELSH PATAGONIANS). Even today Welsh is spoken there. Similarly Cambria was founded in W. Pennsylvania 1794 with chief town Beulah (see WELSH CITY OF BROTHERLY LOVE). In 1850's another Welsh-speaking community was set up in Brazil called Nova Cambria. Other forms of the entry exist like Welsh colonialists and Welsh colonisation. See WELSH SETTLEMENT, WELSH TRACT.

**'Welsh coloured sheep':** A general category of Welsh sheep ('The Western Mail', Sat. 20, September 1997, p.4).

**Welsh Columbus:** Prince Madoc (fl.1170) who sailed to North America over three centuries before Columbus in the 'Gwennan Gorn'. According to legend he married an Indian woman called Zillah. In America there is an organisation called Cymdeithas Madog. Lief Erikson The Viking is also alleged to have discovered Vinland (Wineland = America) before Columbus. See WELSH INDIANS.

**Welsh column:** A section of Welsh news especially in an English paper such as Aneirin Talfan Davies' contributions in The Western Mail (see Stephens ed. 1986:428).

**Welsh comb:** Thumb and forefinger. Similar to the 'llyfiad llo' or calf's lick (licked fingers to arrange front of hair). No relation to a Scotch comb which is a steel comb to dress coat of animals. (A 'Scotch louse trap' is a comb – Green 1996:233). An Irish rifle refers to a small comb.

**Welsh Comet, Ceitho:** A famous WELSH PONY (COB TYPE) foaled 1913 who W. Davies describes as 'a household name in Welsh Cob history' (1993:65).

**Welsh Communitas:** See Trosset's article *Welsh Communitas as Ideological Practice* (Ethos 16(2):66-79,1988). It seems to refer to Welsh community groups.

**Welsh Community Benefit State:** Term used by Hearne for what he envisages as the ideal Welfare State in an independent Wales (1982:212-3).

**Welsh Confederation:** Ken Jones refers to 'Plaid Werdd Cymru's vision of a Welsh Confederation' (Planet 89:115).

**Welsh conical spindle sheaths:** Type of ornate wooden spindle sheath (see Brears 1981-2:34).

**Welsh conjuror:** The 'dyn hysbys' or folk healer/magician who with his crefft y gwynt (craft of the wind) made different swynion or charms to help people. His role was similar to the Cornish 'peller' and Irish 'taman'. Other names were consuriwr (conjuror), swynwr (charmer) and dewin (magician).

**Welsh-conscious:** Conscious of Wales or the Welsh. cf. fashion-conscious.

**Welsh-content:** (of book, material etc.) with contents in Welsh or about Wales.

**Welsh-controlled:** (of authority, organisation etc.) controlled by Wales.

**'Welsh "convert" ':** N. Jones' term for an (English) incomer who by virtue of learning the WELSH LANGUAGE and embracing Welsh culture has become 'Welsh' (1993:127). cf. WELSH BY CHOICE.

**Welsh copper lustre jugs:** A unique Welsh type of jug made by Creigiau Pottery.

**Welsh coracle** (w. cwrwgl): Small type of vessel like a basket covered with hide (perhaps derived from Lat. corium-leather, skin). It is light enough to be carried on the back and used for fishing (see WELSH SEA TROUT). In Wales the two most important types are on the Teifi and Towey rivers. The cwrwglwr is the coracle fisher. The word is a cognate with the longer Irish vessel curragh (yet the Ir. namhag is more similar). See WELSH CORACLE RACING, WELSHPOOL CORACLE.

**Welsh coracle racing** (rasys coryglau): Held during Coracle Week, mid-August at Cilgerran, Dyfed. See WELSH CORACLE.

**Welsh Corgi:** Even though the name 'corgi' (lit. 'dwarf dog') alone seems sufficient, Funk & Wagnalls vol.2 (p.1429) prefix the 'Welsh' as in Cardigan Welsh corgi (long-tailed with rounded ears) and Pembroke Welsh corgi (shorter tail and pointed ears). The breed(s) was/were recognised by the Kennel Club in 1934. The queen has corgis. In Dylan Thomas' 'Under Milk Wood' (1954) Butcher Beynon said he sold cat-meat and corgi-meat (related to the Welsh saying cysgu ci bwtsiwr – a butcher's dog's sleep ie. only a wink, lest he wake up as meat). See WELSH DORGI, WELSH FOXHOUND, WELSH SPANIEL, WELSH SPRINGER SPANIEL, WELSH TERRIER.

**Welsh Cornice:** Two or three oversailing courses of bricks projecting at equal and regular distance to finish with a top. See WELSH ARCH, WELSH VAULT.

**Welsh cornicing:** The making of a WELSH CORNICE (qv.).

**Welsh Coronation Street:** Welsh soap 'Pobl y Cwm' (lit. 'People of the Valley') set in Cwmderin and shown on WELSH FOURTH CHANNEL. With oracle button 888 even WELSHLESS can understand it.

**Welsh corpse bird** (aderyn corff): Like the Cornish tebel edhen (bird of evil omen), a harbinger of death. Usually, like the Greek nekropoúli (or 'death bird') it is associated with the owl. In Funk and Wagnalls we learn that 'In Wales, the hooting of an owl not only presages death but often the loss of virginity of some village maiden' (Leach 1949:838). See WELSH AMBASSADOR, WELSH FALCONER.

**Welsh corpse candle** (cannwyll corff): Briggs (1976:146) prefixes the 'Welsh' and thus it is distinguished from similar foreign lights presaging death as the English fetch candles, Finnish Liekkio and Norwegian Nålys etc. If the flame were small and pale blue a child would die, if large and red an adult and if pale blue, white and large an old sick person. The association of the candle with a soul can be seen in expressions like 'he snuffed it' etc. See WELSH FIERY APPARITION.

**'Welsh Corridor':** A strip of Welsh land surrounded on either side by English/Norman territories (see Mathias 1987:12). See WELSH PEMBROKESHIRE.

**Welsh Cosmopolitanism:** D. Hywel Davis' phrase for Welsh

worldwide context NWR 26:13, Autumn 1994).

See WELSH EUROPEAN, WELSH GLOBAL, WELSH INTERNATIONALIST.

**Welsh costume** (y wisg Cymraeg): Welsh national dress consisting of the WELSH HAT (qv.), pais a betgwn (petticoat and gown – also garb of The Rebeccaites), ffedog (apron) and siôl (shawl). See also WELSH FASHION, WELSH WHISKY, WELSH WIG.

**'Welsh costume dolls':** Phrase used for WELSH DOLL (qv.) in WELSH COSTUME (qv.) in 'The Isle of Anglesey' 1991 Guide (p.30).

**Welsh Cotton:** (Ox.) kind of woollen cloth with a nap. Sutton writes 'This was not a cotton cloth but a woollen fabric . . . produced by a process called 'cottoning' ' (1987:15). See WELSH LINING.

**Welsh cottoning:** The manufacturing of WELSH COTTON (qv.).

**Welsh Court of Great Sessions:** Legal Court in Wales. The Encycl. Brit. says of its extinction in 1830 that it 'served to remove the last relic of separate jurisdiction in Wales itself.'

**Welsh Courts Act** (Oct. 14th 1942): Introduced by Home Secretary Herbert Morrison and stated:

'The Welsh language may be used in any court in Wales by any party or witness who considers that he would otherwise be at any disadvantage by reason of his natural language of communication being Welsh.'

**Welsh cousin:** Rees writes 'The Englishmen's attitude towards kinship is well symbolised by the modern designation of distant relatives as "Welsh cousins" ', (1950:162). See WELSH NIECE, WELSH UNCLE.

**Welsh Craft Fair:** Held at Llandrindod Wells and devoted to unique Welsh crafts eg. WELSH BIBLE BOX, WELSH DRESSER, WELSH LOVESPOONS.

**Welsh Craft Council** (Cyngor y Celfyddydau): It helps

subsidise and promote Welsh crafts.

**Welsh Craft Renaissance:** See WELSH RENAISSANCE.

**Welsh crib:** Goronwy Wyn Evans refers to WELSHLESS politicians giving speeches peppered with Welsh phrases with the aid of a 'Welsh crib' in a waistcoat pocket (Planet 116:125, April/May 1996).

**Welsh cricket:** 1) A louse 2) Tailor. A Scotch grey in Anglo Manx dialect is also a louse. The word 'cricket' has other Welsh associations: Operation Cricket was the greatest ever security in Wales (at the Investiture of 1969). Thompson recounts in the Black Lion pup, Lampeter that men were 'playing a game of "cricket" on the dart board' (1937:115). See WELSH HOCKEY.

**Welsh crowd** (crwth): A native instrument played by a crythor or crowder. It is related to the lyre but its six strings are played with a bow. The cognate Ir. cruit means harp. See WELSH BAGPIPE, WELSH HARP, WELSH HORNPIPE, WELSH VIOLIN.

**'Welsh Cruise'** (Mordaith Bleser Cymraeg): Loffler writes 'Between 1933 and 1939 every Mordaith Bleser Cymraeg ie. Welsh Cruise, took over 500 Welsh speakers to the Baltic and the Mediterranean' (Celtic History Review 1996:8-9). It was organised by Ifan ab Owen of the WELSH LEAGUE OF YOUTH (qv.). cf. WELSH TOUR.

**Welsh C School:** See WELSH CATEGORY A SCHOOL.

**Welsh CSE:** See Welsh GCSE.

**Welsh culm:** Couch says that 'Welsh culm' (dust from WELSH COAL qv.) was used by Cornish farmers to make lime (1871:56). See WELSH STONE.

**Welsh Culture, The Committee for the Safeguarding of** (Pwyllgor Diogelu Diwylliant Cymru): Set up when Welsh was ignored during the war effort (see Humphreys 1973:225).

**Welsh culture, Committee to Defend:** As Ellis (1985:85) translates the above.

**Welsh cupboard:** The American (Webster) name for the WELSH DRESSER. In American English the WELSH DRESSER is also rendered 'hutch' (no relation to WELSH RABBIT, qv.).

**Welsh cupboard-base dresser:** A type of WELSH DRESSER (qv.) with large cupboard bottom as opposed to the open-bottomed WELSH POTBOARD DRESSER.

**Welsh Cup Final:** Since 1990 at Cardiff Arms Park. First won by Wrexham 1978.

**Welsh curate:** C17th saying 'as rugged as a Welsh curate'. Dr Johnson described Evan Evans as 'a drunken Welsh curate' (quoted by Humphreys 1983:81).

**Welsh curd cakes** (cacennau caul Cymreig): A recipe made with curd or cottage cheese, butter, sugar, currants, cake/biscuit crumbs, egg yolks, brandy, lemon rind and shortcrust pastry, (Freeman 1988:35).

**'Welsh currant bread':** As Pugh (1990:45) and others refer to 'bara brith' or 'speckled bread' made with raisins or currants. See WELSH BREAD.

**Welsh D:** See WELSH COB SECTION D.

**Welsh Daffodil** (in Welsh over a dozen names eg. Cenhinen Bedr, 'Peter's Leek' etc.): It is worn like the WELSH LEEK on the breast/lapel by WELSHMEN and WELSHWOMEN on the WELSH NATIONAL DAY. The WELSH CAPITAL is also called 'Daffodil Capital' by Cbers. The Tenby daffodil (Narcissus obrallaris – almost extinct in 1880's when 3½ million bulbs were dug up for London flower stalls) is endemic to Wales (the other common daffodil is also seen in England). Waring writes that 'The Welsh believe it is lucky to find the first daffodil of spring and to do so will bring the finder more gold than silver in the coming twelve months.' (1978:73). Alternatively, 'if daffodils were taken indoors before Easter, the housewife's goose-eggs would never hatch' (Folklore of Blaenau, Gwent 1995:20). See WELSH PATRON SAINT.

**Welsh Daffodil, The True:** As David Jones calls the Tenby

Daffodil (1992).

**Welshdale:** A place name. cf. WELSHPOOL.

**Welsh Day:** Held every year at Westminster. See WELSH DAY DEBATE.

**Welsh Day Campaign:**

**Welsh Day Debate:** Regular annual event in The House of Commons since 1941.

**Welsh 'Dd:** In the WELSH ALPHABET a separate letter pronounced 'th' as in 'then' (as opposed to 'th' which is pronounced as 'th' in 'thing' θ) for which the phonetic symbol is ð. In coelbren, a special symbol ▷ is used instead of doubling d (which is >). No word begins with this letter in Welsh unless it is mutated eg. 'ei ddefaid' (his sheep – defaid is sheep). The letter appears in the middle and end of many words. See WELSH DOUBLE 'L'.

**Welsh Debate:** See WELSH DAY DEBATE.

**Welsh-defying:** (Adj.) of one who defies or resists the Welsh.

**'Welsh deluge Triads':** Category of folk literature mentioned by Rhys (1901:440). See WELSH ATLANTIS, WELSH TRIADS.

**Welsh Demosthenes** (John Elias, 1774-1841): Welsh non-conformist. preacher and reformer so called for his eloquence (Encycl. Brit.). See WELSH BUNYAN, WELSH HORACE, WELSH OVID, WELSH SHAKESPEARE etc.

**Welsh Department** (Adran Cymraeg): Associated with education in Wales.

**'Welsh Derby':** At Chepstow Racecourse on 2nd Tuesday in July (Tucker 1987:42). The Manx Derby was instituted by James Lord Strange at Langness 1628. The Irish Derby is held at the Curragh, Co.Kildare. See 'WELSH NATIONAL'.

**Welsh-derived:** Derived from Welsh. See WELSH LOANWORDS.

**Welsh-descended:** Of Welsh descent eg. 'Welsh-descended Henry Tudor' (Villiers 1965:738). cf. WELSH-BORN.

**Welsh Development Agency** (WDA):

**Welsh Devolution** (trosglwyddiad/cyflwyniad): See WELSH REFERENDUM.

**Welsh Dialect:** A very ambiguous and inaccurate term which has been applied to WELSH ENGLISH (qv.) and the WELSH GYPSY LANGUAGE (Encyc. Brit. qv.). Correctly speaking, the term 'Welsh dialect' should refer to a dialect of the WELSH LANGUAGE. The main variations being North and South Walian each of which have regional sub-dialects.

**Welsh diamond:** A worthless crystal. cf. Cornish diamond – a shiny quartzstone: Bristol diamond – a brilliant crystal of coloured quart from St Vincent's Rock, Clifton; Irish diamond – roch crystal used in watches; Scotch topaz-type of cairngorm stone. See WELSH GOLD, WELSH PEARL, WELSH STONE.

**Welsh diaspora:** See WELSH OVERSEAS.

**Welsh Deirdre:** In Irish Mythology Deirdre was an innocent woman in whose name, others caused bloodshed. In the Mabinogion Branwen was similarly a cause of killing. cf. WELSH HELEN.

**'Welsh Dick Turpin':** Thus Piehler calls Twm Shon Catti (1935:72). See WELSH ROBIN HOOD, WELSH ROB ROY.

**'Welsh Dimension':** Roderick uses this term to describe the residual Welsh element still evident in anglicised areas of Wales (1994:141).

**'Welsh dining club':** G. Evans says of J.E. Jones 'The idea of the Welsh dining club which he established in Cardiff has spread to so many towns . . . ' (1988:325).

**Welsh Dinosaur Agency:** Dylan Iorwerth's satirical allusion to the WELSH DEVELOPMENT AGENCY (Planet 100:107) which he also calls' Welsh Disaster Agency.

**Welsh Disaster Agency:** See WELSH DINOSAUR AGENCY.

**'Welsh Disease':** 1) WELSH NATIONALISM (according to some anti-Welsh people). In the foreward to Hearne's book

(1982) we are told that the author is truly a victim of the 'Welsh Disease' (as our betters in Whitehall laughingly put it). 2) Emyr Humphreys (alias the WELSH MORAVIA) writes that 'The great Welsh disease is threefold like everything else in Celtic Literature: Diffidence, Inertia and Indifference' (NWR 2:11, 1988). cf. WELSH DRUG, WELSH FEVER.

**Welsh Disestablishment Bill:** Introduced by Liberalism 1894 and passed in 1912. See WELSH CHURCH DISESTABLISHMENT.

**Welsh Distributionist League:** See WELSH DISTRIBUTIONIST MOVEMENT.

**Welsh Distributionist Movement:** An extremist group formerly calling itself the Welsh Distributionist League and coming from NF Cymru/Ffrynt Cenedlaethol Cymru, attracting skinheads and 'Welsh' neo-nazi elements, publishing the magazine in English 'The White Eagle' (see G. Davies 1993:77-82).

**'Welsh division':** So Dwyer (1994-95:8) calls 'cyfran' or 'gavelkind', the custom of dividing property equally between children as opposed to primogeniture or leaving just to the eldest son. Although civilized and democratic, this weakened Wales, giving rise to several WELSH PRINCEDOMS and WELSH SUB-KINGS. In an endeavour to unite Wales, Llywellyn Fawr left all the small princedoms to his son Dafydd.

**Welsh Division:** The 38th Welsh Division fought in the Battle of Mametz Wood, Somme, W.W.1. The Welsh Divsion is also the home of WRIS. See WELSH FUSILIERS, WELSH GUARDS, WELSH REGIMENT.

**'Welsh doggis':** Reginald Grey the 'WELSH' MARCHER LORD who provoked the WELSH REBEL HERO Owain Glyndŵr to revolt referred to the Welsh as 'Welch doggis' (quoted in Yr Enfys, Winter 1995/96 p.8).

**Welsh dog kennel dresser:** A type of WELSH DRESSER with an open space at the bottom in the centre (large enough for a dog). Confined to W. Wales where it was known as a 'seld'. The Irish 'hen dresser' kept hens at the bottom. cf. WELSH CUPBOARD, WELSH POTBOARD DRESSER.

**Welsh dog tongs** (gefail cŵn): Used to deter dogs from the church. A pair can still be seen at Clynnog Fawr, Caernarvonshire. In the Isle of Man a 'dog-walloper' had task of driving dogs from church (Andrews 1900). In Ormskirk, Lancashire there was a dog-whipper's bench (Dyer 1892:191-2). In Northorpe Church, Lincolnshire, there was a Hall Dog Pew where dogs were kept during service.

**Welsh doll** (Y Ddoli Gymreig): Though the plastic doll's mostly made in Hong Kong, the WELSH COSTUME the doll wears is often of genuine materials made in Wales. There are many different Welsh dolls each with WELSH HAT and different regional variations of costume.

**Welshdom:** A name for Wales, land of the Welsh. cf. Gaeldom and Taffydom.

**Welsh Donald Duck:** The Welsh cartoon character Wil Cwac Cwac.

**Welsh dorgi:** (No relation to 'dwrgi' – or 'otterboard' with hooks and flies for fishing), the dorgi is a portmanteau of the word daschund and corgi from which the halfbred is derived (see Thurner 1993:43). cf. WELSH HALFBRED, WELSH MULE, WELSH PARTBRED.

**Welsh double chanter:** A variation of a WELSH BAGPIPE with two chanters. It is shown in Woodhouse's book (1995:35).

**Welsh double-cloth coverlet:** Made of two-ply yarn and used for floor rugs (Sutton 1987:62).

**Welsh double 'd':** See WELSH Dd.

**Welsh double-ended spindle sheaths:** See WELSH CONICAL SPINDLE SHEATHS.

**Welsh double hornpipe** (Pibgorn dwbwl): See WELSH HORNPIPE.

**Welsh double 'l':** The Welsh letter 'Ll' which is unique to the Welsh language, for which the IPA had to devise a separate symbol f. It is pronounced like an aspirated 'hl'. See WELSH Dd, WELSH Rh. In coelbren it is N.

**Welsh Dragon** (Y Ddraig Goch): The Red Dragon is the symbol of Wales. Arthur's father Uther (Pendragon) saw a dragon in sky and adopted the symbol. In Merlin's 'The Great Prophecy'the dragomachy between the Red Dragon and White Dragon symbolises the struggle between Wales and England resepectively of which Wales would emerge the victor. In CB language Wales is Dragon Country. See WELSH WINGED SERPENT.

**Welsh drake:** Gadwall, grey duck, german duck (halelusmus streperus). See WELSH AMBASSADOR, WELSH FALCONER, WELSH PARROT.

**Welsh Drama, The Father of:** So Dedwydd Jones calls Twm o'r Nant (the Celtic Pen Vol.2. Issue 1, Autumn 1994). See WELSH SHAKESPEARE.

**Welsh dresser** (y Ddresel Gymreig): A unique piece of Welsh furniture with a large base and shelves on top to display crockery called in America WELSH CUPBOARD (see T.A. Davies 1991).

**'Welsh dresser jugs':** Special crockery for the WELSH DRESSER (B. Lloyd 1945:318).

**Welsh drink:** See WELSH NATIONAL DRINK.

**Welsh Drive:** See WELSH RIDE.

**Welsh Drogheda:** K.O. Morgan describes the scandalous Blue Books (1847) as 'a kind of Welsh Drogheda, a Glencoe and Amritsar of Welsh history' (quoted by W. Gareth Evans, Planet 123:93, 1997). (The English made the parliament of Drogheda forbidden in 1494).

**Welsh Drovers** (Y Porthmyn Cymreig): Men who drove cattle from Wales to England. See WELSH ROAD, WELSH WAY.

**Welsh Drovers' Way:** See WELSH WAY.

**Welsh drug:** Heath refers to Richard Burton being 'addicted to that great Welsh drug, alcohol' (1989:58). See WELSHMAN'S WELSHMAN, WELSH NATIONAL DRINK. cf. WELSH DISEASE.

**Welsh 'D' shaped castle:** Truly Welsh type of castle as distinct from those built by English and Normans (against the Welsh). The tower is D shaped as that of Ewloe Castle near Hawarden, Clwyd, built c.1210 by Llywellyn Fawr.

**Welsh 'D' shaped tower:** See WELSH 'D' SHAPED CASTLE.

**Welsh-dubbed:** (Of a programme) dubbed in Welsh eg. of the western 'Shane'.

**'Welsh Duck':** A casserole recipe of duck, small onions, potatoes, swede, turnip, carrots, fresh herbs, pepper and salt (Smeeth 1994:46). cf. WELSH SALT DUCK. Not to be confused with WELSH DRAKE (qv.).

**Welsh dwarf daffodil:** As the WELSH DAFFODIL is sometimes called. Also simply 'dwarf daffodil'.

**Welshe:** Old spelling of 'Welsh' eg. William Salesbury's 'A Dictionary in Englyshe and Welshe' (1547).

**Welsh Eagle of Snowdon:** Or just 'Eagle of Snowdon' the symbol of the Free Wales Army, the white eagle is derived from the ancient oracle eagles of Snowdonia whose flight showed Welsh victory if they soared high.

**Welsh Earl, The First:** As William, Lord Herbert, Earl of Pembroke (executed 1469) was called (Miles ed. 1994:31).

**Welsh Eastbourne:** Palfrey and Roberts say of Rhyl 'The English translation is "Eastbourne" ' (1994:28). cf. WELSH BLACKPOOL, WELSH MARGATE.

**Welsh Echo:** See WELSH PATRIOT.

**Welshed:** Past tense and past participle of WELSH. Also the adjective referring to a bet/better who has not been paid. cf. Scotched.

**Welsh Eden:** 1) Aaron describes 'the advent of the English tourist to Wales as that of 'a serpent whose poisonous breath' has destroyed the purity of his Welsh Eden' (NWR 27:34, Winter 1994-95). 2) See WELSH GARDEN OF EDEN.

**Welsh Education Act** (1889): Also known as the Welsh Intermediate Education Act which provided education committees in every Welsh county, including Monmouthshire.

**Welshee:** Alternative and slightlier older spelling of WELSHY. Also with the '-ee' stressed in a rising intronotion, a mimic of the WELSH SING-SONG accent.

**Welsh Egon Wertheimer:** K.O. Morgan says of Welsh labour biographers 'we need a Welsh Egon Wertheimer or Maurice Duverger to provide a comparative, analytical treatment' (with reference to the distinguished biographer, NWR 3:37, 1988).

**Welsh eisteddfod:** The word Welsh does not need to be prefixed but 'Welsh eisteddfod' is sometimes met, possibly to distinguish it from the Cornish esethvos and Breton counterpart. The word literally means 'session' (> Welsh eistedd – to sit) and refers to a cultural festival of poetry, song and dance. The two main eisteddfod are the WELSH NATIONAL EISTEDDFOD, held alternately in North and South Wales at a different venue each summer and the International Eisteddfod at Llangollen. Other eisteddfodau were 'tavern eisteddfodau' in pubs, 'eisteddfodau bach y wlad' (small local ones), miners' eisteddfod at Porthcawl, that of the WELSH LEAGUE OF YOUTH and even a Butlins Eisteddfod in early 1950's (see Folk Life Vol.34:18, 1995-96). The eisteddfodwyr are those who go. The highlight is the chairing of the bard. 'Eisteddfoddity' is a neologism (see Gwer.1996:134).

**Welsh ejectment:** To unroof house of tenant to eject him. cf. Kent-street ejectment which is removal of door. The 1996 Fàilte brochure says in relation to the clearances that 'there was an old Highland custom that if tenants had to move from their homes they had to pull down the walls of their home . . . ' See WELSH MORTGAGE.

**Welsh Elderberry Wine** (Gwin Ysgaw): As well as elderberries, seedless raisins and cloves are also used (see Grant 1993:66).

**Welsh Eldorado:** Dowlais. Humphreys says of ap Vychan (Robert Thomas 1808-90) 'at twenty he set out for Dowlais, the Welsh Eldorado' (1983:125). See WELSH ATLANTIS, WELSH GARDEN OF EDEN, WELSH SODOM, WELSH XANADU.

**Welsh Elijah:** Morus Trawsfynydd (Morris from over the mountains) refers to an unexpected guest for whom a place is left (at a wedding). This is perhaps derived from O.T. tradition as the 'kissei shel eliyyahu' (chair of Elijah) is the empty chair at the circumcision. At the Seder/Passover Service the 'kos eliyyahu' (cup of Elijah) is poured and door opened for him to enter. Voth says that at Christmas Poles similarly set an extra place as 'a guest in the house is God in the house' (1983:103). See WELSH MOSES.

**Welsh Elizabethan Catholic Martyrs:** D. Aneurin Thomas' book title (1971). See WELSH CATHOLIC MARTYRS.

**'Welsh elves':** So Briggs (1976:121) and Matthews and Matthews (1988:68) refer to the 'ellyllon' a type of spirit smaller than the 'tylwyth teg' or fairies. See WELSH BANSHEE, WELSH BROWNIE etc.

**Welsh Elvis,** The: Michael Barratt (alias Shakin' Stevens b.1948), very popular Welsh singer once billed as the New Welsh Elvis.

**Welsh embassy:** As Sir J.E. Lloyd (1931:84) calls the French envoys of Owain Glyndŵr who met the French King, Charles VI. cf. WELSH AMBASSADOR.

**Welsh Emigrants Society:** See WELSH EXILES SOCIETY.

**Welsh Emigration Society:** See WELSH EXILES SOCIETY (G. Williams 1991:50).

**Welsh English:** The term can refer to Anglicised Welsh people (WELSHLESS) or their language. By analogy with Chinglish, Hinglish, Spanglish etc. the word 'Wenglish' has been coined (A.T. Ellis 1889:6 quotes John Edwards' 'Talk Tidy') as an alternative to Anglo-Welsh. According to Loreto Todd there are four types of Welsh English: 1) That spoken by bilingual Welsh-people, 2) Dialects of English 3) English with a Welsh accent and 4) R.P. (see McArthur, ed.1992:300).

**'Welsh Equator':** Palfrey and Roberts describe the Landsker (which describes the WELSHRY from Englishry in Pembrokeshire as 'a Welsh equivalent to the Equator' (1994:35).

**Welsher:** The term has several meanings: 1) a Welsh person (eg. Borrow chV) cf. Irisher 2) One who WELSHES A BET cf. Scotcher one who Scotches 3) Man from New South Wales also called WELSHMAN, WELSHIE and New South WELSHER (Waler – refers to an Australian horse) 4) The comparative form of WELSH, ie. 'more Welsh' than – cf. WELSHIER.

**Welsher, New South:** See WELSHER.

**Welsherie:** 1) The practice of a Welsher (old spelling of WELSHERY) 2) Place inhabited by Welsh people cf. Jewerie – inhabited by Jews (see Edwards 1974:21).

**Welsherly:** In the style of a WELSHER (as a distinct from WELSHILY).

**Welsh erotic poetry** (canu maswedd): Type of medieval love poetry.

**Welshery:** 1) The tricks of a WELSHER 2) Area where WELSH SPEAKERS live. See WELSH HEARTLAND.

**Welshes:** Third person singular of the verb 'WELSH' eg. the WELSHER Welshes. A family with supernatural powers in Irish folklore. Wilde (the father of Oscar) wrote: 'everyone knows that the blood of the Welshes, as well as that of the Keoghs and Cahills, beats anything living, except that of a black cat's tail or his lug, for the cure of wild fire . . . A Welsh, by father and mother, would soon be able to eradicate the disease from the whole countryside' (1995:71).

**Welshese:** Slightly pej. term for what seems to be unintelligible language of WELSH SPEAKERS as though something very foreign like Chinese or Burmese. Analogous with Americanese, Australianese, Brooklynese etc. The term could also apply to the speech of WELSH ENGLISH.

**Welshesque:** In Welsh manner or style cf. Arabesque, Bunyanesque (cf. WELSH BUNYAN).

**Welshest** (Cymreiciaf): Most Welsh. cf. WELSHIEST.

**'Welshest of the Welsh':** Frankenberg uses this phrase (copied perhaps by allusion to 'More Catholic than the Pope' etc.) to describe ultra-Welsh characteristics, and applies the appellation to his colleague Emrys Peters (1957:180).

**Welsh Ethnological Studies:** A comparatively new subject discipline taught at the University of Wales, with Trefor M. Owen as Honorary Professor.

**Welsh-ethos:** Ozi Osmond's phrase 'Welsh-ethos education' (NWR 29:92, Summer 1995).

**Welshette:** Humorous term for a little WELSH GIRL. cf. Lawenette – organiser of a 'noson lawen' (Yr Enfys, Winter 1997/98, p.17).

**Welsh Eurocrat:** Glyn Mathias says of Hywel Ceri Jones, Dep. Director of DGS 'After Neil Kinnock he's the most senior Welsh Eurocrat in Brussels' (Planet 122:31).

**Welsh Euro-MPs:** Euro MPs from Wales.

**Welsh European:** The concept of a WELSH PERSON seeing himself in a European context as in John Osmond's book *Welsh Europeans*.
See WELSH GLOBAL, WELSH INTERNATIONALIST.

**Welsh ewe:** See WELSH MOUNTAIN EWE.

**'Welsh Exile':** The term refers 1) to WELSHPEOPLE themselves who are abroad. 2) The actual dispersion of the Welsh (see, for example, Yr Enfys, Winter 1996/97, p.6 and p.8 respectively).

**Welsh Exiles Organisation:** As May calls the WELSH EXILES SOCIETY (qv.) (1994:347).

**Welsh Exiles Society** (Undeb y Cymry ar Wasgar): Society for WELSH PEOPLE who live overseas.

**'Welsh Expatriates, Leader of':** As the president of the WELSH EXILES SOCIETY has been called. Also 'Leader of the Overseas Welsh'.

**Welsh Extremist:** Often pej. term for activist WELSH NATIONALISTS. Ned Thomas with his book *The Welsh Extremist* (1973) has made the term a by-word.

**Welsh-facing:** Facing Wales, as Senior refers to the Mercian dykes (1989:33).

**'Welsh Faggots':** Welsh recipe of pig's liver, onions, shredded suet, breadcrumbs and sage etc. (Howells p.8).

**Welsh Fairies of the Underworld':** So Briggs calls the 'Plant Annwn' (1976:331). See WELSH OTHERWORLD.

**'Welsh Fairy':** In Shakespeare's *The Merry Wives of Windsor* (1957) Falstaff says of Sir Hugh Evans 'Heaven defend me from that Welsh fairy'.

**Welsh fairy costume:** Sikes' term (1880:127,132) for the white clothes of Welsh fairies. In Frennifawr, Pembrokeshire, however, they wore scarlet with red caps.

**Welsh Fairy King:** As A. Jones refers to Gwynn ap Nudd, Brenin y Tylwyth Teg (1995:212). cf. WELSH GOD OF THE UNDERWORLD.

**Welsh Fairyland:** Domain of Welsh fairies. The village of Resolven (formerly Ynysfach) called 'The "Fairyland" of Wales'., home of Wyn ap Nudd (G.F.W.I. 1993:151).

**Welsh Fairy Language:** See WELSH FAIRY-SPEECH.

**Welsh fairy race:** As A. Jones calls the distinct Welsh fairies 'tylwyth teg' or 'bendith y mamau' (1995:434).

**Welsh Fairy-Speech:** The Welsh fairies had their own language, which according to folk tales like Elidor and the Golden Ball had vocabulary like Greek: udrúai – water, halgein – salt etc. T. Gwynn Jones also talks of 'Gaelic elements in Welsh fairy-speech' (1930:73). Apart from their own language, and the WELSH LANGUAGE, Welsh fairies could also understand bees. Indeed bees also understood Welsh (see J.C. Davies 1911:226).

**Welsh faith:** Treachery. cf. Ger. Welsche Treue (J. Green 1996:144. See WELSH BROTH.

**Welsh falconer:** The owl. See WELSH AMBASSADOR, WELSH CORPSE BIRD.

**Welsh fan:** The 'Welsh fan' or Herefordshire fan is a type of corn dolly (see Lambeth 1987:40-2) made from the last sheaf of wheat taken. In Welsh this 'corn dolly' is usually called caseg fedi/y gaseg ben fedi or 'harvest mare' (cf. mare in Hertfordshire). In English Pembrokeshire it is 'neck' (as in Cornwall). The harvest doll is also called 'gwrach' or 'hag' in Wales (cf. WELSH HAG and corresponds with the Highland cailleach or hag). See WELSH BORDER FAN.

**Welsh fashion** (magu yn y siôl): This refers to the method of wrapping a baby inside the 'nursing shawl' or siôl magu. See WELSH COSTUME. Not to be confused with WELSH METHOD.

**Welsh Fasting Girl, The:** Sarah Jacob (1857-69). Little girl who is said to have survived two years without food whose situation parents exploited for publicity. There was also 'Mary Thomas, the Fasting Woman, near Dolgelley' who did not eat nor drink for seven years (P. Roberts 1815:317-30).

**Welsh FDC:** See WELSH STAMPS.

**Welsh featstone** (carreg orchest, maen camp): A large stone thrown as far as possible. Hazlitt (1905:93) describes 'casting of stones' as 'a Welsh custom', yet the sport exists in North England as 'Long Bullets', in Brittany with a 20 kilo stone called 'ar maen'; in Switzerland (see Llafar Gwlad 6:18-19; 8:7), and in the Basque country where the sport is called 'arrijaso keta'.

**'Welsh fetch':** The 'lledrith' which is an apparition of a living person and is a premonition of death.

**Welsh fever:** Term referring to the adulation and admiration of that which is Welsh. It was coined by analogy with Emrys ap Iwan's term Y Dwymyn Seisnig (English fever) to refer to the English-aping mania of many WELSH PEOPLE. cf. WELSH DISEASE.

**Welsh fiddle:** The itch. The same as Scotch fiddle (Anglo-Manx dialect). Wales (and later Scotland) had the nickname Itchland (DHS) and a Scotsman was called on Itchlander. cf. WELSH VIOLIN. See also WELSHMAN'S HUG.

**Welsh Fiddler's Pool:** A stretch of the Severn, more often called just Fiddler's Pool. Palmer writes that the name 'comes from a boat load of Welsh Fiddlers drowned there as they rowed back from over enthusiastic celebrations at Berkeley. On stormy nights their music can still be heard in the wind' (1994:159).

**Welshfield:** A place name.

**'Welsh fiery apparition':** So the 'Tanwedd' is described on the blurb of Hazlitt (1905). See WELSH CORPSE CANDLE.

**'Welsh Fighting Century':** So C19th is called because of the WELSH CHARTISTS (qv.) and the Rebecca Riots (1839) etc. This term is used twice (see Gwer. 1996:135,167).

**Welsh First Day Cover:** See WELSH STAMPS.

**Welsh Fives:** Welsh game of handball (chwarae pêl) or 'ball play' with distinct rules and usually played against church wall on Sunday until bells stopped ringing. In Nelson there is a three-walled court. Despite the name it was played with 2 or 4 players (five perhaps refers to the five fingers – yet in actual fives, ie. non Welsh version eg. at Eton gloves are usually worn).

**Welsh Flag:** 1) The WELSH RED DRAGON flag (the flag of Wales since 1959) 2) A synonym of the WELSH HAG (qv.). See also WELSH FAN.

**Welsh flannel:** Heavy variety of flannel with bluish tinge from Welsh fleeces. There are two types: real Welsh flannel and Rochdale Welsh flannel. The pais fetel is vertically striped flannel for petticoat. 'March the First' is red and black striped flannel, the most famous pattern and used in WELSH COSTUMES on St David's Day. The English word flannel is said to be derived from the Welsh 'gwlanen' (see WELSH LOANWORDS).

**Welsh-flavoured:** Oliver Davies writes 'my teens were spent in Cardiff where . . . it seemed that I was living in a kind of Welsh-flavoured England' (Bowie & Davies, 1992:75).

**Welsh fleece:** Fleece of WELSH MOUNTAIN SHEEP. See WELSH WOOL.

**'Welsh fleece rugs':** One of woollen crafts available from Snail Trail Handweavers, Cilgerran (mentioned in *Mid Wales Festival of the Countryside* guide 1991, p.36).

**Welsh Flyer:** Nothing analogous with the Flying Scotsman but rather the name of a few famous WELSH COBS: eg. Old Welsh Flyer, Young Welsh Flyer, Myrtle Welsh Flyer, Park Welsh Flyer etc. (see W. Davies 1993).

**'Welsh fly-half factory':** Mary Parnell uses this expression to describe the number of great fly halfs/halves Wales has produced, especially with reference to Cliff Morgan and Jonathan Davies (NWR 36:99, 1997).

**Welsh foal:** Foal of a WELSH PONY.

**Welshfolk:** Can be spelt as one word.

**Welsh Folk Dance Society** (Cymdeithas Ddawns Werin Cymru): A society specialises in unique Welsh dances. They organise a Day of Dance. See WELSH JIG, WELSH MORRIS, WELSH REEL.

**Welsh Folk Museum:** See WELSH LIFE, MUSEUM OF.

**Welsh Folk Revival:** Term used eg. by George, Brown & Meazey (1980:3 and back cover) to describe the revival of interest in recent years in aspects of Welsh folk culture such as folk song, dancing and crafts etc.

**Welsh Folk Song Society:** Society which has its own journal and is concerned with unique Welsh songs.

**'Welsh food':** In Cumbria (Wright 1989:18) an in Scots tongue (where it is also Walsh, Wersh, Warsh, Wersh) this is tasteless food.

**Welsh Foreign Legion:** Or simply The Foreign Legion. Like The Jam Boys and The Duffy Taffs, one of the nicknames of the WELSH GUARDS.

**Welsh Forms Act:** Gwynfor Evans (1991:140) mentions 'The Elections (Welsh Forms) Act, since which all official election forms and posters . . . have been bilingual'.

**Welsh Fourth Channel** (S4C): Wales' own Fourth Channel in Welsh, founded after years of petitioning and a hunger strike by leader of the WELSH NATIONALIST PARTY, Gwynfor Evans.

**Welsh 4th Channel:** See WELSH FOURTH CHANNEL.

**Welsh foxhound** (ci hela): A vicious breed of dog with more wiry hair than English foxhound who have been known to eat as well as kill foxes (Encycl. Brit.). Interestingly any dog not a foxhound is called a 'cur-dog' (the etymology of which may be from W. cor – dwarf – see WELSH CORGI). See also WELSH SPRINGER SPANIEL, WELSH TERRIER.

**Welsh Frankton:** A place in Shrops. So called as opposed to English Frankton, 'Welsh Frankton being some five miles nearer to the Welsh border' (Mills 1996:136). cf. WELSH BICKNOR, WELSH MAELOR etc.

**Welsh-free:** (Slightly hum. in reference to programmes, written forms etc.) free from Welsh ie. all in English. cf. sugar free. See WELSHLESS.

**Welsh Free Schools:** As Bennet calls the WELSH CIRCULATING SCHOOLS (qv.) (1962:61).

**Welsh Freedom Fighter:** The term has been used for many WELSH ACTIVISTS of all eras. Freeman describes Owain Glyndŵr thus (1984:5).

**Welsh Friends:** As the WELSH QUAKERS were called (Humphreys 1983:70-1).

**Welsh Frieze:** (Ox.) obs. Term for which meaning is now obscure.

**'Welsh fruitbread':** A category of cake including 'bara brith' etc. Phrase used by Ayto (1994:19).

**Welsh fruit humbugs:** Type of Welsh sweets made by Palls. cf. WELSH MINT HUMBUGS.

**'Welsh furze':** In 1603 George Owen of Henllys wrote 'Another kind of furze there is called small or tame furze, of some, Welsh furze, which is a small and short furze growing on bad ground and never grows to any great height yet serves to bake and brew', (Miles ed. 1994:96). In his note Miles writes 'Tame furze, where "tame" means "dwarf", is ulex galli, which is also known as Welsh furze and as Western gorse. It is low-growing and compact, and blossoms from July to October' (1994:253).

**Welsh Fusiliers,** Royal: Also called Welch Fusiliers. The Museum of the Royal Welch Fusiliers is in Caernarfon Castle, see WELSH GUARDS, WELSH REGIMENT.

**Welsh Fusiliers' Mascot:** A white goat called Taffy, the same as the Royal Regiment of Wales.

**Welsh Gaeltacht:** So the WELSH HEARTLAND (qv.) is sometimes called. See also WELSH LITTLE ENGLAND, WELSH QUARTER, WELSH WALES.

**Welsh Gamaliel:** Humphreys, drawing the analogy from St Paul's mentor, calls Michael D. Jones 'This Gamaliel of Welsh Nationalism' (1983:188).

**Welsh Gammon** (Gamwn Cymru): Siân Llewellyn mentions a recipe of 'Bara Lawr gyda Gamwn Cymru ac wyau/Laverbread with Welsh Gammon and egg' (1974:48). See WELSH HAM, WELSH MUTTON.

**Welsh Gandhis:** Referring to Welsh pacificists, Goronwy Rees wrote in 1964 'It is not likely that Welsh Gandhis or Welsh gunmen will ever set the hearts of their countrymen aflame' (quoted by Stephens ed. 1992:134). Similarly John Davies writes:

'Wedi dyfynnu rhagor o eiriau Mr X am y modd y gellid protestio'n ymarferol, sylw'r gohebydd oedd: "Apparently the role of the Gandhi of Wales will be filled by Mr Saunders Lewis" ' (quoting the Western Mail, 2nd Jan, 1936 from Davies 1981:54). See WELSH HIPPY, WELSH MUSSOLINI.

**Welsh Garden:** Or 'Garden of Wales'. So the Vale of Towy is called (Thompson 1937:152). cf. The Garden of England – Kent.

**'Welsh Garden of Eden':** Humphrey writes cynically about the endangered WELSHNESS 'During the very period which Lloyd George and his generation looked upon as a Golden Age, a veritable Welsh Garden of Eden, the foundation of the whole system was being rapidly eroded' (1983:209). See WELSH EDEN.

**Welsh Garrick:** Williams says of preacher Jubilee Young (1887-1962) noted for his 'hwyl' and entertaining performances, 'In his day he was the Garrick of the Welsh Baptist Circuit' (1973:94).

**'Welsh Gateway':** 1) Or 'The Gateway to Wales'. Abergavenny. 2) According to Piehler 'Bwlch was the Gate of Wales' (1935:67).

**Welsh gathering verbs:** A category of verbs with demutated penultimate consonant and final – eg: afaleua – to gather apples, blawta a blonega (Old Lenten custom of going to houses begging for 'meal and grease'), cawsa (begging for cheese), ceinioca (pennies), gwlana (wool), mela (honey), mesa (acorns), mwyara (blackberries cf. manx smeyney), yta (go Thomasing on 21st Dec., literally to gather ŷd – corn). See WELSH HUNTING VERBS.

**Welsh 'Gaucho':** A Welsh cowboy of Patagonia. cf. WELSH ARGENTINIAN.

**Welsh Gay Capital:** In an editorial, Reeves quotes a Welsh gay short-story magazine 'Queer Words' which calls Aberystwyth 'The Gay Capital of Wales' (NWR 30:7, Autumn 1995). See WELSH BIARRITZ, WELSH CAPITAL.

**Welsh G.C.S.E.:** G.C.S.E. in the WELSH LANGUAGE. cf. WELSH 'A' LEVEL.

**Welsh Gehenna:** In 1841 William Jones described Merthyr as 'The Gehenna of Wales' (quoted by Stephens ed. 1992:41). See WELSH POLITICS, THE CRUCIBLE OF. cf. WELSH SODOM.

**Welsh genealogy, as long as a:** Saying with reference to Welsh interest in genealogies or 'achres' (genealogical table). Vanbrugh in 1697 called Wales 'a country in the world's backside where every man is born a gentleman, and a genealogist' (quoted by Stephens ed. 1992:23). cf. WELSH PEDIGREE.

**Welsh General, Wellington's:** Sir Thomas Picton (shot at Waterloo). From the title of Robert Harvard's book: *Wellington's Welsh General: A Life of Sir Thomas Picton* (1996).

**Welsh Gibraltar:** The Church of England, which in a letter to Queen Victoria 1895, Lord Roseberry said was to Wales 'very much what Gibraltar is to Spain, a foreign fortress placed on the territory of a jealous, pround and succeptible nation', (quoted by Stephens ed. 1992:61). See WELSH CHURCH.

**'Welsh ginger beer** (diod sinsir): Distinct Welsh recipe with not only ginger but dandelions, nettles, rhubarb and blackcurrant leaves (Grant 1993:70).

**'Welsh Gingerbread':** Sold at Welsh fairs and made of flour, bicarbonate of soda, cream of tartar, demerara sugar, butter, candied peel, black treacle and, of course, ground ginger (see Grant 1993:43).

**Welsh Gipsies:** See WELSH GYPSIES.

**Welsh Gipsy Dialect** (Encyc. Brit.): See WELSH GYPSY LANGUAGE.

**Welshgirl:** Written sometimes as one word. cf. WELSHMAN.

**Welsh glaive:** A kind of bill like a pole-axe. See WELSH BILL.

**Welsh glave:** See WELSH GLAIVE.

**Welsh glazed cupboard:** See WELSH DRESSER.

**Welsh Glencoe:** See WELSH DROGHEDA.

**'Welsh Global':** Denzil Davies, writes 'I am not a 'WELSH EUROPEAN' nor a 'WELSH BRITISH' nor a 'Welsh Global'. I am a 'WELSH WELSH' who is proud of the culture, history and language of his country'. (NWR 33:9, Spring 1996). cf. WELSH INTERNATIONALIST.

**'Welsh gloss':** A gloss in Welsh of a manuscript.

**Welsh Gnats:** See WELSH NATS.

**Welsh Gnomic Poems:** The poetical form 'englynion', as in Kenneth H. Jackson's work *Early Welsh Gnomic Poems* (1935).

**Welsh goat:** A nickname in C18th and C19th for a WELSHMAN (DHS). With reference to James Howell's *Party of Beasts* (1660), Mathias alludes to 'Orosian talking goat (that is the Welsh goat) . . . ' (1987:31). According to Sikes 'Welsh goats' had supernatural powers (1880:49, 53-5). See WELSH FUSILIERS MASCOT.

**'Welsh God of the Underworld':** So A. Jones (1995:278) calls Llyr. cf. WELSH FAIRY KING. This epithet could also be applied to Arawn, King of the WELSH OTHERWORLD (qv.).

**Welsh Godfather of Punk:** Welsh-speaker and avant guard musician John Cale (b.1942) who studied in America and with Lou Reed formed group 'The Velvet Underground'. John Cale has been so called since he affected the development of popular music.

**Welsh gold:** 1) Gold from Clogau mine near Dolgellau which is used to make wedding rings for the royal family. 2) Ernest Rhys (1859-1946) poet, novelist and editor, according to his friend Ezra Pound, 'sacrificed a talent for spinning 'Welsh gold' by having to undertake much editing and hack-work' (Stephens ed. 1886:520). cf. WELSH POTOSI.

**Welsh Golden Era:** Thus Hywel Davies describes the late 1960's and 1970's for Welsh rugby (NWR 26:9, Autumn 1994). John Harris refers to the escapism of novels like *How Green was my Valley* as 'a picture of a Welsh Golden Age' (Planet 73:14, 1989).

**Welsh Gomez:** Keidrych Rhys wrote in 1939 that 'Any painter who flatters the features of some Welsh Gomez is always well publicised, and sure of making a living' (quoted by Stephens ed. 1992:98).

**'Welsh Gorsedd':** The meeting of the bards. The word 'Welsh' is not usually prefixed but is sometimes added to distinguish it from other 'gorseddau' (Payton 1996:270) eg. Gorseth Kernow (Cornish Gorsedd). See WELSH EISTEDDFOD.

**Welsh gorsedd motto:** Y gwir yn erbyn y byd (The truth against the world).

**Welsh Gossip Column:** As column of political observer Llygad Llwchwr was dubbed in the London 'News Chronicle', 1950's.

**'Welsh Gothic':** Term used by Schwenk to describe a new genre of Welsh films and with specific reference to 'House of America' (NWR 37:80, 1997).

**Welsh Granary':** Or 'The Granary of Wales' – Anglesey, as it supplied N. Wales with its grain.

**Welsh Grand:** As the WELSH GRAND COMMITTEE is often referred to (eg. by Rosser 1987:74).

**Welsh Grand Committee** (Uwchbwyllgor Cymreig): House of Commons committee est.1960 concerned with WELSH AFFAIRS.

**Welsh Grand National:** See WELSH NATIONAL. cf. WELSH DERBY. The WELSH NATIONAL is sometimes called 'Welsh Grand National' (see for example *Vale of Usk and Wye Valley Guide* p.23).

**Welsh grassland breeds:** Kerry Hill and Clun Forest sheep, as opposed to WELSH MOUNTAIN Sheep. The term is used by Williams-Davies (1981).

**Welsh Greg:** An extinct breed of dog. cf. WELSH HILLMAN.

**Welsh grey face:** See WELSH MULE.

**Welsh Greyhound Derby:** Run at Cardiff 'White City' Sloper Road 1928-44, Cardiff Arms Park 1945-77. cf. WELSH DERBY.

**Welsh Griddle Cakes, Savoury:** Heated on a griddle with

cayenne pepper (Smeeth 1994:12).

**Welsh groin:** An underpitch groin, an intersection of a smaller cross vault with a higher main vault. See WELSH ARCH, WELSH VAULT.

**Welsh groining:** The making of a WELSH GROIN.

**'Welsh Group':** 'One of the oldest groups of exhibiting artists in Wales'. ('Summer Welcome '91: Swansea Bay, Mumbles, Gower' p.12).

**Welsh-grown:** Grown in Wales, eg. 'Welsh-grown wheat' (Freeman 1996:90).

**Welsh Guards** (Y Gwarchodlu Cymreig): Created 1915 and one of the five regiments of foot guards (the others being Grenadiers, Coldstream, Scots and Irish). In WW2 they liberated Brussels on September 3rd. In the Falklands War 39 WELSH GUARDSMEN died on The Sir Galahad. Their uniform is distinguished by a white-green-white plume worn on the left and WELSH LEEK badges. cf. WELSH DIVISION, WELSH FUSILIERS.

**Welsh Guards Band** (Band Y Gwarchodlu Cymreig): The Band of the WELSH GUARDS.

**Welsh Guards Cloister:** Part of The Royal Military Chapel at Wellington Barracks, London. A window of this chapel shows Lawrence Whistler's design of a WELSH DAFFODIL with a view of Harlech Castle within the trumpet.

**Welsh Guardsmen:** Men of the WELSH GUARDS (qv.).

**Welsh Guards Regiment:** See WELSH GUARDS.

**Welsh Guild:** In Philadelphia, U.S.A. an organisation whose 'purpose is to support the Church by acquainting others with the Welsh heritage through Christian fellowship' (Yr Enfys, Winter 1995/6, p.19).

**Welsh Gypsies** (Y Sipsiwn Cymreig): The Gypsies who dwell in Wales. The most famous was Abram Wood whose family were all excellent musicians. See WELSH GYPSY LANGUAGE,

WELSH ITALIANS, WELSH JEWS.

**Welsh Gypsy Dialect:** Term used by Wedeck (1973:498) for WELSH GYPSY LANGUAGE.

**Welsh Gypsy Harpist:** So John Roberts (Telynor Cymru) is called ('English Dance and Song', Vol.56, No.4, Winter 1994, p.20).

**Welsh Gypsy Language:** The distinct form of Romany spoken by WELSH GYPSIES called Romnimos; supposed to be one of the purest forms of Romany.

**'Welsh Gypsy technique':** A term used to refer to a particular style of playing the WELSH TRIPLE HARP (Yr Enfys, Winter 1996/97 p.9).

**Welsh hag:** Type of corn dolly, a literal translation of 'gwrach'. In their entry on 'corn dollies', Beedell and Hargreaves refer to 'Welsh hags and flags' (1979:54). See WELSH FAN.

**Welsh halfbred:** Cross between a border Leicester ram and WELSH MOUNTAIN EWE. cf. Scottish halfbred which is from a border Leicester ram and Cheviot ewe. See WELSH MOUNTAIN, WELSH MULE, WELSH PARK SHEEP, WELSH PART BRED.

**Welsh Halfbred Sheep Breeders' Association:** See WELSH HALFBRED.

**Welsh ham:** (Ox.) Smoked and cured leg of ham. cf. WELSH GAMMON, WELSH MUTTON.

**Welsh Hampton:** Also WELSHAMPTON, a place in Shropshire.

**Welsh Hanging Judge:** Judge Jeffries. See WELSH PARSLEY.

**Welsh harp** (telyn Gymreig): As opposed to the heavy wooden, brass stringed Irish harp or cláirseach, the Welsh harp was always traditionally lighter with strings of horsehair and later gut. The term usually connotes WELSH TRIPLE HARP. Special type of music called 'penillion' and 'cerdd dant' is composed for accompaniment of the Welsh harp. In Welsh mythology

Teirtu had a magic harp which played on its own. cf. WELSH BAGPIPE, WELSH HORNPIPE, WELSH VIOLIN.

**Welsh Harp Building:** In Pontypridd.

**Welsh Harp Conservationists:** An organisation of nature lovers arranging walks in the country etc.

**Welsh harper:** A maker or player of the WELSH HARP. Ellis seems to use this word instead of WELSH HARPIST (1991).

**Welsh Harp Inn:** Name of a famous building.

**Welsh harpist** (telynor, fem. telynores): One who makes or plays the WELSH HARP. cf. WELSH HARPER, WELSH HARP-MAKER.

**Welsh Harp Lake:** A lake in Barry which has been so called because it is shaped like a WELSH HARP.

**Welsh harp-makers:** Even though both terms WELSH HARPER and WELSH HARPIST can connote a maker as well as player, Ellis, to distinguish no doubt from the player uses this term (1991:52).

**Welsh Harp, Queen of the:** So WELSH TRIPLE HARPIST Nansi Richards is called (Sain 1997-1998 Catalogue, p.89).

**Welsh Harp Reservoir** (1834-5): A Reservoir built over the Brent near London and supplying the Grand Union Canal.

**Welsh Harp Society,** North American: A society in U.S.A. which sponsors WELSH HERITAGE WEEKEND.

**'Welsh Harrods':** So Howells, Cardiff has been dubbed (even though it is a chain with a branch in Newport not just one department store). Apparently there is also a 'Falkland Island Harrods' called The Pink Shop.

**'Welsh harvest buns':** Special Welsh buns made with 'glasdwfr', (water and milk) at harvest time (Lady Llanover 1867:478).

**'Welsh harvest mare':** See WELSH FAN.

**Welsh hat** (yr het Gymreig): The tall black hat worn as part of the WELSH COSTUME known variously as the WELSH

CHIMNEYPOT HAT, WELSH BEAVER HAT, WELSH TALL HAT, top hat and WELSH WITCH'S HAT. cf. WELSH WIG, WELSH WISHING CAP.

**'Welsh heads':** The headmasters of Welsh Schools (The Teacher, Jan. 1991). cf. WELSH BLOCKHEADS.

**Welsh-hearted:** With a Welsh heart.

**Welsh Heartland:** Geographically, this can refer simply to the inland regions of Wales or 'Y Berfeddwlad Gymreig'. Culturally it refers to Y Fro Gymraeg. Also called WELSH WALES and refers to the WELSH-SPEAKING regions of Wales – The Pura Wallia which is much of North Wales, parts of the WELSH VALLEYS (qv.) and WELSH PEMBROKESHIRE (qv.) (now part of Dyfed). In other Celtic countries equivalent terms exist. In Ireland the term used is Gaeltacht (whence the expression WELSH GAELTACHT). Strictly speaking, since Irish-speaking areas are scattered along the west coast and reflect regional variations, the plural Gaeltachtaí would be more accurate (as opposed to the Galltacht or English-speaking area(s) ). The Irish even has the term 'Breac-Ghaeltacht' which is an area of mixed Irish and English speakers. Similarly in parts of the Highlands and in the Western Isles there is the Gaidhealtachd (Gaelic-speaking areas). In Brittany there is the Brezhonegva (from which the non-existant Cornish equivalent 'kernewegva' has been coined – by Kendratiev in Carn 83:18, Winter 1993/4). In 'La zone non bretonnante' of Brittany, Gallo is spoken and in Vannes a completely different Breton dialect. There is no Manx equivalent yet the North of the Island (as the extreme west of Cornwall) was the last bastion of the language. Similarly the 'zona euskaldun' is the area of the Basque country where Easkerra/Basque is spoken and 'paises catalans' (as opposed to all Catalunya) are the areas where Catalan is spoken. cf. WELSH LITTLE ENGLAND, WELSH MARCHES, WELSHRY.

**'Welsh Heartland policy':** As Hearnes refers to Clive Betts' ideas of a separated governmental policy concerning industry and education etc. for WELSH-SPEAKING areas. (1982:265).

**Welsh-held:** Held by the Welsh eg. 'Welsh-held castles' (Gater 1991:91).

**Welsh Helen:** 1) Humphreys, with reference to the Dream of Macsen Wledig say it is 'a tale of an emperor who dreamt of a Welsh Helen seated on a golden throne' (1983:28). 2) Also the Helen of Wales: Nest abducted 1109. cf. WELSH DEIRDRE.

**Welsh Hell Hounds:** Pugh (1990:67) calls the cŵn Annwn, the 'Welsh Hell Hounds'. Other Welsh names of these ill omened dogs of Gwyn ap Nudd, King of Annwn are Cŵn Cyrff (corpse dogs), Cŵn Wybr (sky dogs), Cŵn Toili (WELSH PHANTOM FUNERAL dogs), Cŵn Bendith y Mamau (fairy dogs), gwyllgi (wild dog), cŵn wyler and cŵn duon (black dogs). They hunt at night are frightful in appearance and a premonition of death. Other parts of Britain also have hell hounds eg. The Devil's Dandy dogs and Cheney's hounds in Cornwall etc. cf. WELSH BANSHEE, WELSH WATER HORSE.

**Welsh Heptarchy:** Historical term pertaining to the organisation of Wales into seven countries C9th-11th.

**'Welsh Herald Extraordinary':** As Morris calls Owain Glyndŵr (1995:31).

**Welsh Heritage Week:** Held by some WELSH AMERICAN societies.

**Welsh Heritage Tour:** Annual tour organised by WELSH AMERICANS from U.S.A. to Patagonia. cf. WELSH TOUR.

**Welsh Hermits favourite Chicken and Leek Pie:** Recipe recorded by Lady Llanover (1867:445).

**'Welsh Herrings':** A recipe of herrings baked with apple, potatoes, onions, sage and butter (M. Williams 1994:30).

**Welsh Highgrove,** The: Morris writes hypothetically of a Prince of Wales which some Welsh royalists would like:

'Perhaps Cardiff Castle could be made over to the Prince, as a building that is historically neutral . . . or perhaps he could acquire a Welsh Highgrove, a country house where he could live in a style suitably Welsh, surrounded by Welsh-speaking staff, honouring Welsh traditions' (1995:28).

**'Welsh high hat':** Term used in index of Plomer (1944:349) for the WELSH HAT even though Kilvert's actual entry of 14th Oct. 1870 refers to a 'tall Welsh hat'.

**Welsh High King** (Brenin Pennaf): Equivalent of the Irish Ard Ri and Saxon Bretwald and refers to a king of all Wales, the last of which was Gruffydd ap Llywellyn (see G. Evans 1988:37 and Jackson 1989:26 (GW). cf. 'WELSH DIVISION', WELSH PRINCE, WELSH SUB-KING.

**Welsh Highland Plateau:** (Encycl. Brit.) See WELSH HIGHLANDS.

**Welsh Highland Railway:** A mountain railway opened 1980.

**Welsh Highlands:** In 1773 Rhys Jones wrote that the Welsh were 'driven by the Saxons from the Lowlands of England to the Welsh highlands' (quoted by Stephens 1992: 29). cf. Scottish Highland; White Highland (European area of Kenya). See WELSH ALPS, WELSH MATTERHORN, WELSH RABBITS, SOCIETY OF, WELSH SUB-ALPS, WELSH 3,000S, WELSH TIGER.

**Welsh Highland Wool:** See WELSH MOUNTAIN WOOL.

**Welsh hill:** Type of Welsh sheep. See WELSH MOUNTAIN.

**Welsh Hillman:** Not any Welsh make of car but an extinct breed of dog. cf. WELSH GREG.

**Welsh hill speckled face:** Type of Welsh sheep (see Williams-Davies 1981:32).

**Welsh hippy:** Making a pun on the name of the great Saunders Lewis, Dylan Iorwerth mentions 'an old Welsh hippy called Sandals Lewis' (Planet 103:111, Feb-March 1994). See WELSH JOKE.

**'Welsh historical romance':** A genre of Welsh fiction (Bell's term NWR 4:75, 1989). See WELSH INDUSTRIAL NOVEL.

**'Welsh hobby horse':** Thus Simpson calls the 'Mari Lwyd'

(1976:170) or horse's head covered by a sheet and taken from house to house during the Christmas season. Peate says the name means 'grey mare' (not Grey Mary) and corresponds with the Irish hobby horse 'Láir Bhán' (white mare) (1963:95). The Mari Lwyd is accompanied by characters like Punch and Judy (Pwnsh a Siwan), Meriman etc. Other names are Y Warsel, Y March or Y Gynfas Farch (see Alford 1978:64). The hobby horse is found in many countries outside Wales. See WELSH WATER HORSE.

**Welsh hockey:** Bando. A game played with a club called a (pren) bando in C19th Wales with many each side distinguished by different coloured ribbons. cf. WELSH CRICKET, WELSH POLO, WELSH WRESTLING.

**'Welsh hogswash':** So metheglin, the WELSH NATIONAL DRINK was described by the English (G.H. Jenkins 1996:8).

**Welsh holiday homes:** See WELSH SUMMER HOUSES.

**Welsh Holy Mountain:** Skirrid Fawr, mountain near Abergavenny which according to legend slipped at the moment of the crucifixion (hence the name from ysgyryd – 'separate'). cf. The Holy Mountain – Athos, a community of Orthodox monasteries in N. Greece.

**'Welsh Holywood':** Title of article referring not to films about Wales made in Holywood (eg. 'How Green was my Valley') but Holywood films made in Wales (such as 'First Knight' and 'August' with Anthony Hopkins). (Yr Enfys, Winter 1995/6, p.17).

**'Welsh Homer':** 1) Not so much an epithet but the title of a poem by James Cliff (Planet 11:27-8). 2) Piehler says of Taliesin 'He may . . . be a sort of Welsh Homer, ie. a mythical figure to whom a mass of contemporary and later poetry has been ascribed' (1935:130). 3) Wintle writes that R.S. Thomas 'is like Homer in a thousand fragments, shorn of narrative concern' (quoted in NWR 36:82, 1997). cf. The Gaelic Homer-Ossian, The English Homer-Milton etc. See WELSH HORACE, WELSH MARTIAL, WELSH OVID, WELSH VIRGIL.

**Welsh Home Rule** (Ymreolaeth hunan-lywodraeth): The complete independence of Wales advocated by Cymru Fudd and now by the WELSH NATIONALIST PARTY. See WELSH PARNELL.

**'Welsh Home Rule Party':** An ideal party suggested by Arthur Price which would reflect WELSH NATIONALIST interest instead of being dependent for very modest concessions from the Liberals (quoted by G. Evans, 1974:414).

**Welsh home ruler:** A supporter of WELSH HOME RULE.

**Welsh Home Service:** Type of Welsh Broadcast in early days before BBC Wales. See WELSH FOURTH CHANNEL.

**Welsh homespun cloth** (brethyn cartref or brethyn talpentan or 'fire-back cloth'): Natural material for WELSH COSTUME also called 'Welsh homespun'. See WELSH COTTON, WELSH FLANNEL, WELSH LINING.

**Welsh Honours List:** Margaret Jones says of the WELSH GORSEDD: 'Its extending of honorary membership to those who have served Wales and her culture . . . may also be considered an uniquely Welsh form of 'Honours List' ' (1986:31).

**Welshhood:** The state of being WELSH.

**Welsh hook:** The 'Welch hook' was a kind of bill (axe with two edges). An old rhyme says:
    'A salmon, cor, or chevin,
    Will find you six or seven
    As taull man as ever swagger
    With Welse-hooke, or lang dagger.'
See WELSH BILL, WELSH GLAIVE.

**Welsh Hook:** A place south of Fishguard.

**Welsh hooke:** See WELSH HOOK.

**Welsh Horace:** Borrow in his 'Wild Wales' (Ch. LXXXVI) says of Dafydd ap Gwilym (fl.1320-70):
    'He was something more than the WELSH OVID;

he was the Welsh Horace, and wrote light, agreeable, sportive pieces, equal to anythings of the kind composed by Horace in his best moods. But he was something more: he was the WELSH MARTIAL, and wrote pieces equal in pungency to those of the great Roman epigrammalist – perhaps more than equal.'

According to Brewer the Horace of England was George, Duke of Buckingham, The Horace(s) of France – Jean Macrinus and Pierre Jean de Béranger (also the French Burns), The Horace(s) of Spain – The de Argensola brothers. cf. WELSH SHAKESPEARE.

**'Welsh horn':** The white horn of WELSH MOUNTAIN rams which is less large and twisting than horns of other breeds and it is best suited for the carved handle of shepherds' sticks (Jones and Owen 1996:20,40).

**Welsh hornpipe** (y pib-gorn Cymreig): Unique Welsh wind instrument. cf. WELSH BAGPIPE, WELSH DOUBLE HORNPIPE, WELSH HARP, 'WELSH VIOLIN'.

**Welsh Horse Fair:** So the Barnet Fair/Ffair Barnet is called.

**Welsh horse-wedding** (priodas geffylau): At the priodas fawr (great wedding) parties were on horseback and guest contributed. cf. 'shigowts' at which women were on horseback in wedding procession. The custom is not confined to Wales.

**Welsh hose:** See WELSHMAN'S HOSE.

**Welsh hound:** See WELSH FOX HOUND.

**Welsh Household Spirit:** As A.Jones (1995:86) describes the 'bwbachod' a sort of WELSH BROWNIE who plays destructive pranks and performs household talks. He dislikes teetotallers and non-conformist minister. Ellis describes him as the 'Welsh household sprite' (1992:54). cf. WELSH BANSHEE, WELSH CHANGELING.

**Welsh Huddersfield:** According to the National Museums & Galleries of Wales brochure, The Museum of the Welsh Woollen Industry at Dre-Fach, Felindre once had forty mills and was called 'The Huddersfield of Wales'. cf. WELSH LEEDS.

**Welsh hug:** See WELSHMAN'S HUG.

**Welsh Humanists:** (Stephens ed. 1986:152).

**Welsh hunting verbs:** Like WELSH GATHERING VERBS, formed from the noun plus final – 'a' and includes fishing verbs eg. eoca (catch salmon), llygota (catch mice), llymrieita (catch sand eels), llysgwenna (catch eels). cf. Breton – broc'heta – hunting badger.

**Welsh hurling:** 'Bando' has often been described as 'a sort of Welsh hurling' ('Folklore of Blaenau, Gwent', 1995:19).

**Welshiana:** See WELSHANA.

**Welchicide:** Or Cymricide. The killing of that which is Welsh, especially the WELSH LANGUAGE. cf. The 'linguagide' of Celtic language(s) (McArthur 1992:203).

**Welshicise:** Cymricise, to make WELSH.

**Welshiciser:** One who WELSHICISES.

**Welshicising:** Making WELSH. cf. G. Evans uses term 'Cymricising' (1988:161).

**Welshicism:** That which has been made/created WELSH. cf. WELSHISM.

**Welshicist:** A WELSHICISER. cf. WELSHIFIER.

**Welshicity:** An unsatisfactory alternative to WELSHNESS. Perhaps coined from 'Welsh ethnicity'?

**Welshicize:** See WELSHICISE.

**Welshicization:** The making WELSH of something. WELSHIFICATION. cf. Hearne uses the word 'Cambricisation' (1982:265).

**Welsh-identified:** Identified as Welsh. David Lloyd describes some poets thus (Planet 121:107). See WELSH-IDENTIFYING.

**Welsh-identifying:** John Barnie describes Planet's 'Welsh-identifying profile' (Planet 117:3); Ned Thomas speaks of a

'Welsh-identifying private sector' (Planet 122:121).

**Welshie:** cf. Scotchie (Anglo. Manx for a Scotsman). A WELSHPERSON or thing. cf. WELSHEE, WELSHY.

**Welshier:** More WELSHY than. cf. WELSHER.

**Welshiest:** The most WELSHY. cf. WELSHEST.

**Welshifiable:** That which can be WELSHIFIED.

**Welshification:** The making WELSH of something. cf. WELSHICIZATION.

**Welshified:** Made Welsh, eg. Bobi Jones says of some WELSH PEOPLE 'Their Welsh becomes anglicised, and their English . . . is too Welshified' (Planet 22:57, March 1974).

**Welshifier:** One who makes WELSH.

**Welshify** (Cymreigeiddio, Cymreigio): To Cymrise or make WELSH. The Welsh term applies specifically to changing/translating into Welsh.

**Welshifying:** Making Welsh eg. inside cover of Parry-Jones (1964) talks of games 'subsituting Welsh terms for the English and 'Welshifying' the others'.

**Welshifyingly:** Adverb of WELSHIFYING.

**Welshikins:** A little WELSHCHILD. cf. WELSHLING.

**Welshily:** Especially in the expression 'to go/travel Welshily'.

**'Welsh imperialism':** Term mentioned by Bob Jones (Planet 22:63).

**Welsh Independence, 1st War of** (1276-7): See WELSH WARS.

**Welsh Independence, 2nd War of** (1282-3): See WELSH WARS.

**'Welsh Independent, The First':** As G. Evans calls John Penry (1563-93) Protestant evangelist and writer, hanged for his faith.

**Welsh Independent TV:** See WELSH FOURTH CHANNEL.

**Welsh Indians** (Yr Indiaid Cymraeg): When Madoc went to America he is said to have married an Indian girl called Zillah. John Evans in C18th later found 'Welsh-speaking Indians' (The

Mandans) some of whom had blue eyes. These 'Welsh Indians' or 'Madogwys' did not really speak Welsh yet their language had several Welsh words or words similar to Welsh: glas (blue in both languages), bara (bread), jurig (boat) – like the WELSH CORACLE, pan-head (pen in Welsh) etc. (See Berlitz 1983:197). In Mobile Bay, Alabama, there is a plaque in honour of Madoc who 'left behind, with the Indians the WELSH LANGUAGE'. See WELSH COLUMBUS, WELSH-TEHUELCHE.

**'Welsh Indian Theory':** So De Camp calls the theory that identifies the Mandans with the Welsh (1970:124). See WELSH INDIANS, WELSH-SPEAKING DOEG TRIBE.

**'Welsh industrial novel':** A particular genre of Welsh and Anglo-Welsh literature. The term comes from the name of Raymond Williams' work (1979) and refers to novels set in Wales dealing with the 'industrial experience' of the working class Welsh. This (sub-)genre of Welsh novel is exemplified in the works of Alexander Cordell, but also the classic *How Green Was My Valley* and even several contemporary novels in this vein.

**Welshiness:** The characteristic/quality of being WELSHY. cf. WELSHNESS.

**Welsh-influenced:** Influenced by Wales or by that which is Welsh.

**Welshing:** Gerund or continuous form of WELSH. The word 'Welshing' is now being replaced with other words by ITC writers and even President Clinton has been criticised for using it (see Wales Review, August 1996, Issue 1, p.58). See WELSHER. cf. Greeking – cheating at cards (DHS).

**Welshingly:** Adverb of WELSHING, ie. done in the way of a WELSHER.

**Welsh-inspired:** Inspired by Wales or the Welsh. cf. WELSH-LED.

**Welsh Intermediate and Technical Act** (1889): See WELSH EDUCATION ACT.

**Welsh Intermediate Education Act** (1889): See WELSH EDUCATION ACT.

**Welsh international:** One who plays rugby for Wales internationally.

**Welsh Internationalist:** 1) An epithet for the magazine Planet; 2) A Welshperson with an international outlook, eg. D.R. Barnes refers to Gwyn A. Williams (1925-95) as 'The quintessential Welsh internationalist' (Planet 115:126, Feb./March 1996). See WELSH EUROPEAN, WELSH GLOBAl.

**Welshisable:** See WELSHIFIABLE.

**Welshise:** To make WELSH.

**Welshiser:** One who makes something WELSH.

**Welshish:** Similar to WELSH – as opposed to WELSHY.

**Welsh islands:** There are many islands off the shores of Wales, the most important of which is Anglesey (Ynys Môn). Other islands include Bardsey, Caldy, Ramsey, Stokholm, Skomer etc. which are bird sanctuaries and old monastic sites. In Welsh Mythology there were also the Islands of the Blessed etc. See WELSH CINCINNATUS, WELSH GRANARY, WELSH STOCKHOLM, WELSH VOLE.

**Welshism:** Cymricism. Use of a Welsh expression in English. cf. Irishism etc.

**Welshist:** A supporter/advocate of what is Welsh. Perhaps coined by analogy with Welsh + racist.

**Welsh-Italians:** Also Italo-Welsh and refers either to Welsh of Italian extraction eg. opera singer Adelina Patti (d.1919) or those of mixed Welsh and Italian parentage. From late C19th Italian immigrants came to South Wales and after WW2 many Italian POWs remained. Many established themselves as café owners or restraunteurs. See Basini (1992). cf. WELSH GYPSIES, WELSH JEWS.

**Welshite:** A nickname for a WELSH PERSON. cf. Israelite etc.

**Welshitis:** (Hum.) sickness caused from that which is WELSH.

cf. other neologisms like 'telephonitis' borrowing the suffix '-itis' used for medical complaints eg. apendicitis, tonsilitis etc.

**Welshize:** See WELSHISE.

**Welsh Jack the Ripper:** In the 1997 Countryside Books Complete Catalogue, Paul Harrison's *South Wales Murder Casebook* is described as 'A collection of murder stories including one about the Jack the Ripper of Cardiff'.

**Welsh Jacobins:** Republicans influenced by The French Revolution.

**'Welsh Jane Eyre':** Thinking of a version palatable to the Welsh, Jane Aaron writes 'I'm afraid that a Welsh Jane Eyre would have to choose St John Rivers rather than Rochester as her husband if she was to retain her readers' sympathies' (NWR 38:41, 1997).

**Welsh Jeckyl and Hyde:** Swansea. Thompson, thinking of the city's contrasts wrote 'Swansea – The Jeckyl and Hyde' (1937:31).

**Welsh Jews:** Jews from Wales. Apart from the distinct Jewish minority in Wales, WELSH PEOPLE have always had an affinity with the Jews eg. Hebrew names for Welsh Chapels like Sion. In 1804 John Evans stated that Welsh was a dialect of Hebrew. Indeed Welsh, like Hebrew has been dubbed 'The Language of Heaven' and the WELSH LANGUAGE REVIVAL has used the Wlpan system (> Heb. Ulpan Akiva). In the film 'Elizabeth Taylor' (1995) Richard Burton tells Liz' previous (Jewish) husband that the Welsh are one of the lost tribes of Israel. Thompson (1937:236) saw a WELSH GIRL from Cricieth who told him 'Jones isn't a Welsh name . . . Jones is Jewish'. See Abse (1993:16-21). cf. WELSH ELIJAH, WELSH MOSES.

**Welsh Jig:** Type of dance, Welsh variation of jig. cf. WELSH REEL.

**Welsh 'Jock':** Someone of mixed Welsh and Scots parentage.

**Welsh 'Joe Public':** Thus Dai Woosnam refers to the average Welsh reader or member of the Welsh public (NWR 26:83).

**'Welsh Johnnies of Dossen',** The: Phrase used by G. Griffiths (1987:119) with reference to WELSHIFIED Johnnies eg. Joseph Olivier in Brittany (as opposed to Breton Johnnies in Wales).

**Welsh Joint:** Short for the WJEC (Welsh Joint Education Committee) or CBAC (Cyd-Bwyllgor Addysg Cymru), the examining board in Wales who organise examinations in English and in WELSH. See WELSH A LEVEL, WELSH GCSE, WELSH O LEVEL.

**Welsh Joint Education Committee:** See WELSH JOINT.

**Welsh Joke:** According to Gwyndaf (1993-94:80) a unique and definite category of joke. Welsh humour is distinct and noted 'for quaintness and sentimentality' (McArthur, ed.1992:381). Just as Scotsmen joke about Aberdonians, and Irishmen about Kellymen, so Welsh joke about the 'Cardi' (supposedly mean person from Cardiganshire). 'Hanner Cardi' is someone who is a half-Cardi. Gerald of Wales extols Welsh humour (p.243). Richards shows Welsh sexual jokes as subtle but not crude (1993:28-9) and observes that the butt of many Welsh jokes is the Englishman (1993:7). See WELSH BOOMERANG, WELSH HIPPY, WELSH MUG.

**Welsh Jonah:** See WELSH SAVONAROLA.

**Welsh Jumpers:** No relation to pullovers (see WELSH SWEATER) but a nickname for the WELSH PRESBYTERIANS (qv.) or WELSH CALVINISTIC METHODISTS who jumped with fervour at meetings.

**'Welsh junta':** Petro's phrase to describe those who ran the mines in the WELSH ATHENS (Scranton). See WELSH STRIKE (1994:108).

**Welsh keffel:** William Hutton wrote in 1803 that 'a Welsh Keffel will climb almost as well as his master' (quoted by Kirk 1994:122). He was referring to a horse, possibly a WELSH PONY. The word 'keffel' is a WELSH LOAN WORD (qv.) and exists in the English language (Chambers etc.) with the meaning 'horse, nag'. It is, of course, derived from the Welsh word for horse 'ceffyl' (cf. the cognates: Manx 'cabbyl', Fr. 'cheval', Sp. 'caballo', It. 'cavallo', etc. from the Latin 'cabullus'. See WELSH WATERHORSE.

**'Welsh kilt':** Peate wrote in 1972 (p.64) of 'a small band of misguided folk who attempt to 'revive' (as part of a non-existent 'national dress') a Welsh kilt!' No doubt he would be saying the same about the Cornish kilt today. WELSH TARTAN (qv.) is different from the tartan 'setts' in Highland and Irish kilts. cf. WELSH COSTUME, WELSH FLANNEL, WELSH TWEED.

**Welsh King, Cathedine:** One of the greatest WELSH PART-BRED HORSES.

**Welsh kingdoms:** Domains of Welsh kings as opposed to the smaller WELSH PRINCEDOMS.

**Welsh King Lear:** Llŷr – father of Manawydan (cf. Ir. Manannan mac Lir), Brân (see WELSH ULYSSES) and Branwen in the Mabinogion.

**Welsh Kiwi:** A New Zealander of Welsh extraction.

**Welsh knockers:** Potter's phrase (in Funk and Wagnalls) for the mine spirits: 'Welsh knockers were alleged to be 18 inches high' (Leach 1949:585, p.585). See WELSH MINE GOBLINS.

**Welsh knot:** See Welsh Not.

**Welsh 'kulturkampf':** Baker, referring to the literary background of Caradoc Evans and contemporaries' who initiated a kind of Welsh 'kulturkampf' against its ethical pedantry and prurient moralising' (1995:9). W. Wynn Thomas used the same term about Caradoc Evans' *My People* (NWR 1:18, 1988).

**Welsh-L:** Refers to 'Welsh-L internet' and 'Welsh-L subscribers' (D. Lloyd & Planet 116:77). For cars Welsh prefer 'D' (Dysgwr) than 'L' for 'Learner'. See WELSH DOUBLE 'L'.

**Welsh    :** Phonetic symbol for WELSH DOUBLE 'L'. Not to be confused with the Polish 't' which is pronounced 'w'.

**Welsh Labour Action:** Internal pressure group calling for a powerful WELSH PARLIAMENT on a par with what Labour was offering Scotland.

**Welsh Labourism:** Policy of close co-operation between Welsh Labour Party and WELSH NATIONALISTS.

**'Welsh lacquer':** As M.E. Jones calls William Allgood's Japanware of Pontypool (1978:122).

**Welshlad:** (One word).

**Welshlady:** Can be written as one word.

**Welsh lamb:** Smaller and with sweeter meat than English or New Zealand lamb. Found in phrases like WELSH LAMB ENTERPRISE. Most Welsh recipes (see following recipe entries) require exclusively 'Welsh lamb' from WELSH MOUNTAIN sheep for that unique Welsh flavour and texture. 'Swci' is a pet lamb. See WELSH MUTTON.

**Welsh lamb, Crown Roasf of** (Coron Oen Cymru wedi'i Rostio): Dish of roast lamb decorated when served with cutlet frills resembling a crown (S. Llywellyn 1974:74). It is served with a variety of vegetables.

**Welsh lamb, Honeyed** (Oen Cymreig Melog): Spring dish of WELSH LAMB prepared with honey and rosemary (Freeman 1988:11).

**Welsh Lamb Pie:** Pie made with neck of WELSH LAMB, parsley and carrots (Grant 1993:16).

**Welshland:** Like Manxland (for the Isle of Man), Welshland has been a slightly humorous term for Wales, conjuring up ideas perhaps of its 'primitive' background analogous with names like Somaliland, Bechuanaland in Africa and Maoriland (for Maori-populated parts of New Zealand). cf. Aussieland. See WELSHLANDER. cf. Cymland (perh. Cymru + land??) is the title of a children's book by Robat Gruffudd (Y Lolfa). Other names are Itchland (see WELSH FIDDLE) and Taffyland.

**Welsh Land Commission:** Est. by Gladstone to publish report of Welsh rural life in 1896.

**Welshlander:** Name for a WELSH PERSON. cf. Scotlander and Irelander (Iain C. Uallas uses terms in Carn. 95, 1996:4); Aussielander. See WELSHLLAND.

**Welsh Land League:** A Body formed in 1886 concerned with Welsh land. Led by Tithe War activist Thomas Gee.

**'Welsh Land's End':** The Llŷn Peninsula. Thomas calls it the 'Land's End of North Wales' (1990:61). Snowdonia is also so-called (Pen Tir Cymru) in *Wales: A Tourist Guide to Crafts and Places to visit.* (Official Guide: Wales Tourist Board, Ch.9).

**Welsh Land Tenure Commission** (1893): Commission apointed by Lord Roseberry's cabinet whose report (pub. 1896) exonerated squirearchy from charges of extortion and sectarian oppression.

**'Welsh lane':** A green, country lane or road (Ox.).

**Welsh Language** (Cymraeg): Like Cornish and Breton, a member of the Brythonic branch of Celtic Languages. From late C6th Early Welsh emerged from the original Brythonic Celtic language of Britain. The language is phonetic and unique (like fellow-Celtic languages) in that it experiences mutations (qv. WELSH MUTATIONS). In contrast with English, the Welsh language has changed comparatively little through the centuries; modern WELSH PEOPLE are able to read medieval Welsh quite easily. Due to the WELSH NOT and English domination etc. the number of Welsh speakers was reduced dramatically. Now less than 20% of WELSH PEOPLE speak WELSH as their mother tongue. See WELSH HEARTLAND etc.

**Welsh-language:** (adj.) Refers to literature, education courses, visual material, programmes etc. in the WELSH LANGUAGE.

**Welsh Language Academy** (Academi Iaith Cymru): Proposed by J. Elwyn Hughes at the Eisteddfod Genedlaethol, Castell Nedd to invent Welsh words for new concepts instead of copying English terms (based on the French Academy / Académie Française and their purist language policy).

**Welsh Language Act** (1967): Permitted Welsh in legal

proceedings (qv. WELSH COURTS ACT, 1942) and allowed bilingual signs, making Welsh and English of equal status in theory. The Welsh Language Act of 1993 reconstituted The WELSH LANGUAGE BOARD.

'Welsh-language activity holidays': Phrase to describe holiday courses to learn Welsh at centres like Nant Gwrtheyrn (eg. phrase used by N. Jones 1993:137).

**Welsh Language Bandits:** Dylan Iorwerth's name for the WELSH LANGUAGE BOARD (Planet 107:110). See WELSH LANGUAGE BAWD.

**Welsh Language Bawd:** Dylan Iorwerth's jocular homophone for the WELSH LANGUAGE BOARD (Planet 107:110). See WELSH LANGUAGE BANDITS.

**Welsh Language Bill** (1967): See WELSH LANGUAGE ACT.

**Welsh Language Board** (Bwrdd yr Iaith Gymraeg): F.1988 to promote WELSH LANGUAGE.

**Welsh Language Centre, National:** In Nant Gwrtheyrn.

**Welsh Language Circle** (Cylch Cymraeg Tocio): A Welsh Society founded in Japan by Breton Laurence John.

**Welsh-Language Civil Rights Movement:** As Cefn is sometimes called (May 1994:84). See WELSH CIVIL RIGHTS MOVEMENT.

**Welsh Language dormitories:** Dormitories exclusively for Welsh-speaking students eg. at Bangor and Aberystwyth. Trosset uses phrase (1993:59).

**Welsh Language Lecture, Annual** (Y Ddarlith Flynyddol Gymraeg): Held in the Cardiff Literature Festival in Autumn.

'Welsh-language Mafia': John Bradbury, expressing S. Walian views of 1979 said that 'a WELSH ASSEMBLY would become the bastion of a Welsh-language mafia . . . ' (quoted by Roger Dobson in *Independent on Sunday*, 14 Sept. 1997, p.17). See WELSH MAFIA.

**'Welsh language matters':** How Carys Moseley translates 'Y Pethe'. (Planet 125:123, 1997).

**Welsh Language Service:** See WELSH FOURTH CHANNEL.

**Welsh Language Society:** (Cymdeithas yr Iaith Gymraeg): Founded in 1962 to safeguard the WELSH LANGUAGE. Prior to the WELSH LANGUAGE ACT many activist members defaced roadsigns. Over 1,000 members have been imprisoned. In 1971 some members broke away to form Adfer ('restore') to concentrate on WELSH in the WELSH HEARTLAND.

**Welsh Language, Society for the Utilisation of the:** A society founded in 1885 whose Welsh name was Cymdeithas yr Iaith Gymraeg (name later used by the WELSH LANGUAGE SOCIETY, qv.).

**Welsh Language Sunday Schools:** As the WELSH SABBATH SCHOOLS (qv.) are sometimes called (eg. by G. Evans 1974:347).

**Welsh Language toys:** Category of toys made to facilitate the learning of Welsh (M.E. Jones 1978:24,87,160).

**Welsh Language Week:** See WELSH LANGUAGE WEEKEND.

**Welsh Language Weekend:** Weekend organised for WELSH LEARNERS to enable them to have opportunities to practise their WELSH.

**Welshlass:** (Can be written as one word); see WELSHGIRL.

**'Welsh Last Movement':** Eleri Carrog writes: 'we have "Welsh Last" movements set up in Dyfed called "Education First", to prevent WELSH MEDIUM education affecting their children'. (NWR 15:16, Winter 1991/92).

**Welsh law code:** See WELSH LAWS.

**Welsh laws** (Cyfreithiau Cymreig/Hywel) Leges Walliae/Britannia. Like the Brehon Laws in Ireland, The Laws of Hywel Dda (The Good) (d.950) were native to Wales. See WELSH WEREGILD.

**Welsh lay:** (Ox.) a class of roofing slates. cf. WELSH RAG, WELSH LUMP.

**Welsh League of Youth** (Urdd Gobaith Cymru lit. Welsh League of Hope): In a letter written in January 1922 Ifan ab Owen Edwards had idea to form an Urdd Gobaith Cymru Fach (League of Hope of Little Wales). Due to the great response from young people, the 'little' was soon dropped. It is indeed often referred to as simply the 'Urdd' and this organisation has organised its own eisteddfodau, Urdd Sunday and 'mabolgampau' games. See WELSH CRUISE.

**Welsh Lear:** See WELSH KING LEAR.

**Welsh Learner of the Year:** Competition introduced in 1983.

**Welsh Learners** (Dysgwyr): The term refers almost exclusively to learners of the WELSH LANGUAGE for whom classes are held, special magazines like 'Prentis' are published and events like the WELSH WEEKEND are held. As regards Welsh learner drivers, the 'D' (Dysgwr) plate is preferred to the 'L' plate. See WELSH LEARNERS PAVILION.

**Welsh Learners' Council:** As CYD is called (eg. by N. Jones 1993:137).

**Welsh Learners Pavilion** (Pabell y Dysgwyr): The special pavilion at the eisteddfod for WELSH LEARNERS to meet, chat and with specially graded events and talks (> W. pabell - tent, cf. Ir. puball).

**Welsh Learners Society** (Cyngor y Dysgwyr): Society founded in 1984 for the benefit of WELSH LEARNERS.

**Welsh Learners Tent:** An alternative name eg. as M. Jones uses (1986:45) for the WELSH LEARNERS PAVILION.

**Welsh-learning:** (adj.) That which relates to the learning of Welsh. eg. Welsh-learning books, material and programmes.

**Welsh-led:** Led by Wales or the Welsh. In *Guilty men* by Spy No.3 Dr Thomas Jones, C.H. we read of 'The Welsh-led and WELSH-INSPIRED General Strike of 1926' (Quoted by Gwer.

1996:50).

**Welsh Leeds,** The: As Jenkins tells us 'Newton, the centre of the (textile) industry, was known to early nineteenth century travellers as "The Leeds of Wales" ', (1985:5). cf. WELSH HUDDERSFIELD.

**Welsh Leek** (cenhinen pl. cennin): Like the WELSH DAFFODIL the leek is the other WELSH NATIONAL SYMBOL or WELSH NATIONAL EMBLEM. According to 'Byegones' (Sept.6, 1899) the Welsh were infested by Orang Outangs so they invited English to exterminate them. The English not being able to distinguish the Welsh from the apes killed WELSHMEN too so told them to wear leeks to be identified (quoted by Holland 1992:11). Apart from the means of identification Waring says that Welsh warrior rubbed their bodies with leeks 'because they believed it gave them extra strength in battle and prevented them getting wounded' (1978:140). The custom of wearing a leek on St David's Day is alluded to in Henry V – Gower asks Fluellen: 'But why wear your leek today? Saint Davy's day is past.' Hazlitt believed wearing a leek derived from the cymhortha (neighbourly aid) when it is a custom for each individual to bring his portion of leeks (1905:165). On Saint David's Day a new officer of the WELSH REGIMENT must eat a raw leek and quaff a pint of ale in one draught. The leek is also used in many Welsh recipes and was the diet of Welsh Saints. In May each year there is a leek-throwing competition in Crickhowell. See WELSH MUG, WELSH PATRON SAINT.

**Welsh Leek Broth:** A type of leek soup (recipe of Lady Llanover 1867:451).

**Welsh leeke:** Old spelling of WELSH LEEK.

**Welsh Legionnaires:** As Miles calls the contingent of WELSHMEN who belonged to the Roman army. Some left with Magnus Maximus (1969:179). See WELSH FOREIGN LEGION.

**Welsh leg of mutton:** See WELSH MUTTON.

**Welshless:** A literal translation of the Welsh 'di-Gymraeg' as in Cymro di-Gymraeg (Welshless Welshman) to describe a Welshman who does not speak Welsh. cf. Breton 'divrezhonek' meaning non-Breton speaking but also anti-Breton. Similarly 'euskaldunmotz' in the Basque term for a Basque who does not speak his own tongue. See WELSH HEARTLAND, WELSH MONOGLOT.

**Welsh-less:** Hyphenated form of WELSHLESS used by some eg. J.P. Clancy (NWR 38:90, 1997).

**'Welsh Liberation':** Welsh independence. The Lolfa catalogue describes D. Hearne's book *The Joy of Freedom* as the basis for an 'Ideology of "Welsh Liberation" '

**'Welsh lickspittles':** WELSH PEOPLE who are toadies to the English rulers. 'The modern Welsh lick-spittles and time-servers' (Gwer. 1996:112). cf. 'Welsh boot-lickers' (ibid. p.50).

**Welsh Life, Museum of** (Amgueddfa Werin Cymru): New name for the WELSH FOLK MUSEUM in St Fagans.

**'Welsh light cakes':** See WELSH CAKES.

**Welshlike:** That which resembles something WELSH. cf. WELSH-LOOKING.

**Welsh lily:** The daffodil (see WELSH DAFFODIL).

**Welsh lilly:** See WELSH LILY.

**Welsh-lilted:** (Of a voice) with a Welsh accent.

**Welshling:** A little WELSH PERSON. cf. WELSH PRINCELING.

**Welsh lining:** Woollen cloth with nap. cf. WELSH COTTON.

**Welsh Listeners' Society:** Est. in 1950's by J.E. Jones. They refused to pay licence fees for BBC radio when the few Welsh programmes were transmitted on inaccessible wavelengths.

**Welsh literary Renaissance:** See WELSH CLASSICS.

**'Welsh literati gliterati':** Dylan Iorwerth's phrase for Welsh 'authors and budding-writers' collectively (Planet 73:106,

Feb/March 1989).

**Welsh Little England:** Or 'Little England Beyond Wales'. So the area south of WELSH PEMBROKESHIRE is called, ie. south of the Landsker. The term is particularly applied to the Flemish-descended community of Tenby. See WELSH HEARTLAND.

**Welsh Little Holland:** Or simply 'Little Holland', an area of Gwent (see G.F.W.I. 1994:13).

**Welsh Little Switzerland:** The Afan Valley. There is a Little Switzerland in London. Similarly Kashmir is India's Switzerland and Singapore is the Asian Switzerland etc. cf. WELSH ALPS.

**Welsh Liverpool:** Or Liverpool Welsh. There is a large Welsh community in Liverpool, hence the epithet 'Capital of North Wales' (qv. WELSH CAPITAL).

**Welsh Ll:** See WELSH DOUBLE 'L'.

**Welsh loanwords:** The term refers to those English words that are WELSH-DERIVED: bodkin – a small dagger (> coch a bon ddu – red with black stem), cromlech, cwm, eisteddfod, flannel (see WELSH FLANNEL), flummery, tinker (according to Hunt 1881, vol.1:66 > W. tincian – to ring), skipper – barn (R.D. vol.3:1292) (> W. ysgubor). Additionally there are false etymologies like pengwyn (white head) (for penguin) which has a black head and obviously not a true loan word. See WELSH KEFFEL.

**Welsh London:** London Welsh. There is a large Welsh community in London, particularly active with cultural societies. See WELSH SCHOLARS.

**Welsh Londoner:** A London Welshman. cf. WELSH COCKNEY.

**Welsh longbow:** According to Gerald of Wales was 'made of wild elm, unpolished, rude and uncouth', faster than a crossbow and could pierce a mail hauberk'. See WELSH BOWMEN. cf. WELSH BILL, WELSH GLAIVE.

**Welsh long bow:** See WELSH LONGBOW.

**'Welsh long-bow archers':** As the WELSH ARCHERS (qv.) are sometimes called (eg. by G. Evans 1974:243,250).

**Welsh longbowmen:** See WELSH BOWMEN.

**Welsh long-house:** Spelling of WELSH LONG HOUSE (qv.) used by some writers eg. E. Wiliam (1992).

**Welsh long house:** Unique type of Welsh building (see John 1976:5) with dwelling house (pen uchaf) at north end and cowhouse and stable at lower end (pen isaf) separated by a feeding walk/passage called y penllawr. See WELSH ROUND HOUSE.

**Welsh-looking:** (adj.) That which looks Welsh.

**Welsh Lourdes:** The holy well of St Winifride was called by Dr Johnson in 1774 the 'Lourdes of Wales' (see WELSH WONDERS). cf. Knock, Co. Mayo which since 1879 has been called 'The Lourdes of Ireland'.

**Welsh Lovers, Patron Saint of** (Nawddsant Cariadon Cymru): As Gwyndaf calls St Dwynwen (1989:37/33). See WELSH ST VALENTINE. cf. WELSH PATRON SAINT. See also WELSH LOVE SPOON.

**Welsh love spoon** (llwy garu/serch): A wooden spoon made by a man for his 'cariad', hence the word 'spooning'. There may be many different symbols: eg. a bell (for church wedding), a spade (I will work for you), anchor (security) etc. Sometimes little balls (peli/sfferau) are carved inside the neck of the spoon and their number represents the desired number of children. Collectors may like to display them on a special car llwyau or spoon rack. The largest collection is in the Brecknock Museum. In Scotland a man bought silver spoons for his fiancée (Guthrie) 1885:45). See Stevens (1993:133-8). cf. WELSH SPOON CARVER, WELSH ST VALENTINE.

**Welsh-loving:** (adj.) (Of someone) who loves Wales and the Welsh.

**Welsh lump:** 1) Fire brick made in large pieces. The same as the

Stourbridge lump. 2) A name for the WELSH NOT (qv.).

**Welshly:** In a Welsh way. cf. WELSHILY.

**Welsh lynching:** Ellis (1989:220) quotes the Oswestry Advertizer 1880 which refers to 'the old Welsh form of lynching called "cludo ar ysgol" (to carry the ladder) in which the victim is seized, strapped lengthways on a ladder and carried or jolted through the place'. See WELSH SKIMMINGTON.

**'Welsh lyric poetry':** Dafydd Johnston's term to describe the poems of Ieuan Glan Geirionydd (Evan Evans 1795-1855) and Alun (John Blackwell, 1757-1841) (1994:72).

**Welsh Maelor** (Maelor Gymraeg): One of two commotes of Powys, the other being English Maelor (Maelor Saesneg).

**Welsh Maen:** An old spelling of the WELSH MAIN (qv.). See P. Roberts (1815:216-7).

**Welsh Maffia:** See WELSH MAFIA.

**Welsh Mafia:** No relation to the WELSH TRIADs but the Taffia – the nepotistic network of prominent WELSH PEOPLE. By coincidence WELSH MAFIOSO Llewelyn Morris Humphreys (The Hump/Camel) from Carno, Powys was Al Capone's right hand man and Public Enemy No.2 (see Yr Enfys, Spring 1994). In addition to the Taffia, there is by analogy the 'Murphia' 'applied to a group of Irish broadcasters prominent in the UK in the 1980's' (Isaacs & Law eds. 1994:416). See WELSH LANGUAGE MAFIA, WELSH OLD BOYS' NETWORK.

**Welsh Magic, Brynmor:** A famous WELSH COB.

**Welsh Maid:** The name of a few famous WELSH COBS: eg. Teifi Welsh Maid, Cathedine Welsh Maid and Meiarth Welsh Maid.

**Welsh main:** As opposed to the equally barbaric 'battle royal' in cockfighting where all cocks were put into the pit to fight until one remained as victor, the Welsh main was a 'tournament' at which sixteen cocks were pitted in eight pairs, then the eight victors in four fights and so on. In Cumbria the same cruel 'sport' was called the stagmain, 'stag' meaning 'cock' (Rollinson 1987:168). In the MUSEUM OF WELSH LIFE is the cockpit from the Hawk and Buckle Inn, Denbigh, Clwyd.

**Welsh mainland:** Wales proper, as opposed to the WELSH ISLANDS.

**Welsh main-land:** See WELSH MAINLAND.

**Welsh male voice choir** (Côr Meibion [Cymry]): Probably male voice choirs originated in Wales. Gerald of Wales noticed that whereas the English sang in unison, the Welsh sang in different parts with a harmony.

**Welshman** (Cymro): 1) One word cf. Irishman, Scotsman. As in Gerald the WELSHMAN. An older spelling is Welchman (eg. Hazlitt 1905:88). cf. WELSHMAN. 2) Effigy of a Welshman hanged in London in the time of Pepys. Also called 'Taffey, Taffey' or 'David, David'. 3) In parts of the Carribean a 'Welshman' or 'Wenchman' is 'a pink or reddish fish with large, black eyes and a prominently bony dorsal fin; it weighs about 2 lbs' (Allsopp 1996:595). 4) 'Welshman' is also the name of the jabbering crow of Jamaica because of its guttural sounds (J. Green 1996:62 cites Edward Lang's *History of Jamaica*, 1774).

**Welshman, 'good':** Usually the Welsh 'Cymro da' is preferred and refers to a WELSHMAN who is good as regards his political loyalty to Wales.

**Welshman', 'honorary:** A non-Welshman can become thus by eating a leek with the Royal WELCH FUSILIERS (Planet 117:82).

**Welshman, 'The little':** The way many referred to Lloyd George (Mile 1969:166). See WELSH WIZARD.

**Welshman, The Wild** (Cymro Gwyllt): Richard Jones (1772-1833) hymn-writer.

**'Welshman by choice':** See WELSH BY CHOICE.

**'Welsh Mandans':** As Berlitz (1983:197) calls the WELSH INDIANS.

**Welshman Hall Gully:** Also Welchman Hall Gully, a gully in Barbadoes. cf. WELSHMAN'S GULLY.

**Welsh-mania:** See WELSHOMANIA.

**Welshman's button:** Or Halford's Welshman's Button (Trichoptera: seicostoma personatum) a caddis fly. The 'Welshman's button', like the WELSH PARTRIDGE and WELSH SHRIMPFLY is used for fishing. No relation to 'Irish button' which is syphilis (J. Green 1996:257).

**'Welshman's cow', little and good like a:** A saying (Grenfell-Hill quotes a headmaster who liked to use the phrase in early C20th, 1996:25). cf. WELSHMAN'S PRICK, SHORT AND THICK LIKE A: WELSH-SPEAKING COW.

**Welshman's Fields:** Colyer, referring to the routes used by WELSH DROVERS writes that 'A "WELSH ROAD" passed through Staffordshire, Warwickshire and Buckinghamshire; a 'WELSH WAY' bypassed Cirencester in Gloucestershire, while 'WELSHMAN'S PONDS', 'WELSHMAN'S FIELDS' and various corruption of WELSH words occur regularly in field and place names' (1984:116).

**Welshman's Gully:** Place in South Island, New Zealand where gold was discovered. See WELSH GOLD. cf. WELSHMAN HALL GULLY.

**Welshman's hose:** To make a Welshman's hose of, turn anything to a Welshman's hose or make like a Welshman's hose means to turn something anyway to suit one's purpose. cf. Shetland hose is a stocking made of Shetland wool.

**Welshman's hug:** An itch, the same as WELSH FIDDLE. Green tells us that 'in the county of Somerset any form of venereal disease is known as Welhsman's hug' (1996:257). cf. A Cornish hug is a move in Cornish wrestling (see WELSH WRESTLING); A Scotchman hugging is a clusia or type of W. Indian creeper (DHS).

**'Welshman's Party', The:** As Hearne describes the Labour Party in the minds of many Welsh voters (1977:94).

**Welshman's Ponds:** See WELSHMAN'S FIELDS.

**Welshman's prick, short and thick as a:** An old expression. Other racist comments in relation to this part of the anatomy are Irish root – penis, Irish toothache –priapism; and Jewish nightcap – foreskin (DHS).

**Welshman's Welshman:** So Richards (1993:40) refers to Richard Burton because 'behind the voice was a man of obvious intelligence, passion and character'.

**Welsh-Manx:** That which relates to both Wales and the Isle of Man.

**Welsh March:** See WELSH MARCHES.

**Welsh Marcher Lords:** A misnomer since they were English/Norman Lords of the WELSH MARCHES.

**Welsh Marches** (Y Gororau > W. goror – border): Marchia Wallie (as opposed to Pura Wallia). Like the 'Debatable Land' on The Scottish/English border, this land was contested by both Welsh and Normans. Some were ruthless eg. William de Braose (The Ogre of Abergavenny – see WELSH NIGHT OF THE LONG KNIVES). Owain Glyndŵr began his WELSH REVOLT when a Marcher Lord stole his land. cf. La Marca Hispánica (The Spanish March = Catalonia). See WELSH BORDER.

**Welsh mare:** A WELSH PONY mare. A mature female WELSH PONY or WELSH COB. W. Davies tells us that at one time there was a trend to mate 'Welsh mares' with Arab and thoroughbred horses for a 'new' Section B. cf. WELSH PART BRED.

**Welsh Margate:** Rhyl. Thompson, in N. Wales quotes the epithet of Rhyl as 'The "Margate" of this coast' (1937:244). See WELSH BIARRITZ, WELSH BLACKPOOL, WELSH RIVIERA.

**Welsh Marie Celeste:** Palfrey and Roberts say of Llandrindod Wells 'There are people still actually living there but to the inexperienced eye it is the veritable Marie Celeste of Wales' (by allusion to the 'ghost ship', 1994:74).

**Welsh Martial:** 1) Dafydd ap Gwilym. See WELSH OVID. 2) John Owen (1564?-1628?) epigrammist called 'The British

Martial'. cf. WELSH BUNYAN, WELSH SHAKESPEARE.

**Welsh Matrons, Coven of Formidable:** As Palfrey and Roberts describe Merched y Wawr (Women of the Dawn) (1994:48). Sounds more like a female relation with WAWR!

**'Welsh Matterhorn:** (Yr Enfys, Spring/Summer 1995:p.4). Or 'The Matterhorn of Wales': Cnicht. Yet Barber (1992:106-7) compares the Skirrid (see the WELSH HOLY MOUNTAIN) with the Matterhorn. See WELSH ALPS, WELSH HIGHLANDS, WELSH RABBITS, SOCIETY OF, WELSH SUB ALPS, WELSH 3,000s.

**'Welsh mat-makers':** Those who make mats from 'mor-hesg', a sea-reed which grows on the 'twyni' (sand dunes) (A.M. Jones 1927:78).

**Welsh Mazzini:** Tom Ellis (1859-99), politician and supporter of WELSH HOME RULE who was influenced by the philosophy and idealism of the Italian Mazzini.

**Welsh-medium:** Through the medium of Welsh (trwy y gyfrwng Cymraeg), especially of education.

**Welsh Medium Comprehensive** (Ysgol Gyfun): A Comprehensive School in which all lessons are taught through the medium of Welsh.

**Welsh Medium Education, Parents for** (RhAG – Rhieni Dros Addysg Gymraeg): Association concerned with WELSH-MEDIUM education. See WELSH NURSERY MOVEMENT.

**Welsh Medium Nursery Schools and Playgroups, The National Association of** (Mudiad Ysgolion Meithrin): See WELSH NURSERY MOVEMENT.

**Welshmen** (Cymry): (One word) cf. WELSHMAN. An old spelling in 1494 was Walshemen (Hazlitt 1905:169).

**Welsh-mens:** Old C17th genitive form of WELSHMEN, hyphenated and without apostrophe (Hazlitt 1905:169).

**Welshmen, Seven Jolly:** See Welshmen, Three Jolly.

**Welshmen, Three Jolly:** Game in which one child acts as an employer and others, coming to him for work, mime their job which the employer must guess (Parry-Jones 1964:106-7).

**Welshmen in Dispersion, Society of:** See WELSH EXILES SOCIETY.

**Welsh Merit Table, Whitbread:** A ranking system.

**'Welsh method':** Puddling, ie. the converting of pig iron into maleable iron by decarbonizing it (J.G. Jones 1990:103). cf. WELSH PROCESS, WELSH-WROUGHT.

**Welsh Methodism:** See WELSH PRESBYTERIANS.

**Welsh Methodist Revival:** See WELSH REVIVAL.

**Welsh Methodists:** See WELSH PRESBYTERIANS.

**Welsh Metropolis:** 1) Or 'Metropolis of Wales', an epithet for Cardiff since 1873 (see also J. Wilson 1996:15,20). 2) G. Evans describes Ludlow as a 'Welsh Metropolis' (1974:319) because of the Council there in the first half of C17th. See WELSH CAPITAL.

**Welsh Midlands:** Central Wales.

**Welsh mile:** A mile or more, a tedious journey (Ox.). 'Like a Welsh mile, long and narrow' a C18th saying. Like a Yorkshire way-bit (distance greater than a mile). In 1701, E.B. (probably Edward Bysshe) wrote in 'A Trip to North Wales' that 'our next day's journey . . . consisted of 12 Welsh (that is to say 36 English) miles: for every one of them was a complete Dutch League' (quoted by Kirk 1994:42). This would make a Welsh mile – 3 miles. Similarly there was an Irish mile ('a mile plus', DHS), a Cornish mile – 2240 yards, a Scots mile – 1976 yards, a Scandinavian mile – 6 miles. Perhaps the discrepancy can be explained by the etymology of mile > Lat. milia > millie – 1,000 (ie. paces). However, elsewhere we are told that 'In Wales, one mile = 4 English miles' (Hosier 1984:550).

**Welsh Military Dragon:** Lofmark (1995:43) refers to this particular dragon symbol which was used by Welsh warriors. See WELSH DRAGON.

**'Welsh Militia':** With reference to the organisation of WELSH SETTLERS in Patagonia, Ellis writes 'The Welsh Militia were better disciplined and trained than the Argentine troops sent against them' (1985:176).

**Welsh Miltonic:** H.T. Edwards (1990:13) says of Goronwy Owen (1723-69) that his 'ambition to write a Welsh Miltonic, Christian epic had been frustrated by the inadequacy of the twenty four strict metres'.

**Welsh-minded:** (adj.) With a Welsh mind. cf. bloody-minded, open-minded. cf. WELSH-HEARTED, WELSH-THINKING.

**'Welsh Mine Goblins':** As Briggs calls the 'coblynau' (1976:77) who are little spirits who live in mines. They are the equivalents of the Cornish knockers (hence also called WELSH KNOCKERS, qv.), the English blue-cap, the German kobold and the Gypsy 'cameni micuti' (Wedeck 1973:57). Other names for them in Wales are Tylwyth teg y mwn (fair folk of the mine) (Sikes 1880:12) and cnocwyr mewn pyllau mwyn (mine knockers). cf. WELSH BANSHEE, WELSH BROWNIE, WELSH CHANGELING, WELSH WATER HORSE etc.

**Welsh Miner's Debate** (1912): Term (K.O. Morgan 1995:ch7) referring to syndicalist thinking of leaders such as Ablett and Cook as opposed to conciliatory views of older miners.

**'Welsh mining town-that-was-mad':** As John Harris calls Cwmglas, setting for the gothic thriller *The Three Weird Sisters* (film script by Dylan Thomas) (Planet 117:109).

**Welsh Mint:** Place where coins were minted in Wales (alluded to by M.C. Harris 1980:51).

**Welsh Mint Humbugs:** Type of Welsh sweets manufactured by Palls.

**Welsh miracle plays:** Term used (Stephens ed. 1986:596) for only two surviving C16th works: Y Tri Brenin o Gwlen (the Three Kings of Cologne) and Y Dioddefaint a'r Atgyfodiad. There are more extant examples of Cornish miracle plays (Corn. gwary myr/myrakl).

**'Welsh mischievous spirits':** As A. Jones (1995:212) calls the 'gwyllion' – hideous female fairies who (like Cornish pigsies) make travellers lose way. If a knife is held to them they are thwarted. The 'gwyllion' are associated with goats and can take goat form.

**'Welsh mist':** Borrow (ch.XVII) wrote 'The mist soon wetted us to the skin not withstanding that we put up our umbrellas. It was a regular Welsh mist, a niwl, like that in which the great poet ab Gwilym lost his way . . . ' Indeed this unique Welsh meteorological phenomenon (similar to 'Scotch mist' [which also means a sarcastic retort or whisky and lemon]) inspired the mystery for the 'beirdd y niwl' (poets of the mist – alias, T. Gwynn Jones & W.J. Gruffydd). In the romance of Geraint and Enid a 'hedge of mist' guards a field of games from which no one who enters can return. cf. Ir. Ceo-druidechta (druid fog) which covered with invisibility.

**Welsh Model:** Name of two famous ponies: Neuadd Parc Welsh Model a WELSH PONY COB-TYPE filly foal which cost 1,700 guineas in 1989. Mabnesscliffe Welsh Model a WELSH COB filly foal was sold for a record of 4,800 guineas in 1991.

**Welsh mole trap:** A unique and nasty Welsh trap used by the 'gwaddotwr' or 'tyrchwr' (mole-catcher). Meredith Morris referred to 'the old Welsh mole trap with an ∧ shape pin called a 'bradwr' which the mole touched . . . with its nose, thus releasing the string holding down the spring and compassing its own death' (1910:38).

**Welsh Monarchy Society:** A short-lived organisation founded by Keith Griffiths and Anthony Lewis (in late '60's) to try to cater for prospective WELSH NATIONALIST members of royalist persuasion (see Clews 1980:94).

**Welsh monoglot** (Cymro di-Saesneg): A WELSH-SPEAKER who cannot speak English. Perhaps amongst the WELSH PATAGONIANS, it could technically refer to a WELSHPERSON, in particular a very small child who has not yet learnt Spanish. Elias (1987:41) quotes the 'Farmers' Magazine' (1856) in which there was an allusion to 'an-English-speaking Welshmen'. cf. WELSHLESS.

**'Welsh Monoglottism':** The ability to speak only Welsh by WELSH SPEAKERS. N. Jones argues that 'Welsh Monoglottism is the only answer to English monoglottism' (1993:153).

**Welsh Moravia:** With reference to the Italian novelist Alberto Moravia (dubbed the 'Italian Balzac'), M. Wynn Thomas writes 'Bearing in mind that Italy is Emyr Humphrey's second home, it might be not altogether inappropriate to dub him "The Moravia of Wales", in recognition of the scope and scale – and – yes, the "relentlessnes" of his achievement' (NWR 13:37, 1991).

**Welsh Mormon Exodus:** As Ronald D. Dennis calls the wave of emigration of Welsh Mormons from 1849 to Utah (Planet 73:39-45, Feb-March, 1989). This exodus was also a loss for the Welsh language since many of the mormon emigrants were Welsh-speakers. cf. 'WELSH SAINTS'.

**'Welsh Morris':** A distinct type of Morris dancing performed in Wales and similar in form to Chesire and Derbyshire forms (T.M. Owen: 1959:93). See WELSH JIG, WELSH REEL.

**Welsh Mordecai:** G. Evans writes 'The function of the Welsh M.P. now was to support Lloyd George – 'our Mordecai', as one of them called him' (1974:421). The allusion is to the adoptive father of Esther whose counsel saved the Jews. See WELSH BARD, WELSH WIZARD.

**Welsh mortgage:** 'Mortgage in which the lender takes a conveyance of the property and rents and profits from his possession instead of interest on the loan; it is redeemable at any time on payment of the loan and the mortgage is unable to compel redemption or force closure' (R.D. 1202). This was derived from the ancient legal practice called 'prid' which Carr describes as 'a mortgage that was never redeemed' (1979:22). cf. WELSH EJECTMENT.

**Welsh Moses:** The poet Taliesin (fl. late C6th). Like Moses (who was put into a basket on the Nile), so Taliesin was cast by Ceridwen into the sea in a coracle (see WELSH CORACLE) and was found by Elffin ap Gwyddno Garanhir, who, like the Egyptian princess who found Moses, renamed the child from Gwion Bach to Taliesin. See WELSH PHARAOHS.

**Welshmost:** The most Welsh. In Nigel Jenkins' poem 'Byzantium in Arfon', he writes:

'The conquerors' first, most counter-Welsh of towns, this

Constantinople of the western vertex

Where Rome ends and the Raj begin

Is by now the Welshmost town in Wales . . .' (Planet 121:25)
cf. WELSHEST, WELSHIEST.

**Welsh motto:** 'Cymru am Byth'. (Wales for ever).

**Welsh Mountain:** Native Welsh sheep who are known in breeds such as Black/Welsh Mountain, Hardy Welsh Mountain and Improved Welsh Mountain. Their meat is excellent (see WELSH LAMB), as is their wool (see WELSH WOOL) and also their horns are used for craftwork (see WELSH HORN). The term could also be applied to breeds like South Wales Mountain and Defaid Torddu (Badger-faced sheep). See WELSH HALFBRED, WELSH MULE, WELSH PARK SHEEP etc.

**Welsh Mountain-bred sheep:** Phrase used by M.E. Jones (1978:95) for WELSH MOUNTAIN Sheep.

**Welsh Mountain ewe:** Mated with a border Leicester ram for a WELSH HALFBRED. cf. WELSH RAM.

**Welsh Mountain pony:** Smallest breed of native WELSH PONY descended from the original Celtic pony which existed over 1,000 years ago. See WELSH MOUNTAIN PONY SECTION A.

**Welsh Mountain pony Section A:** In the WELSH PONY AND COB SOCIETY and competitions and events such as the ROYAL WELSH AGRICULTURAL SHOW, it is the smallest category of WELSH PONY used mainly for children and should not exceed 12hh ('hands' ie. 122cms). cf. WELSH PONY SECTION B, WELSH PONY OF COB TYPE SECTION C,

WELSH COB SECTION D.

**Welsh Mountain School of Fiction', 'Myfanwy of the:** Sally Robert Jones' term for stereotype Welsh fiction for children (NWR 8:6, 1990).

**Welsh Mountain sheep:** See WELSH MOUNTAIN.

**Welsh Mountain Sheep Society:** Est. 1905.

**Welsh Mountain spiderwort:** Or simply 'mountain spiderwort' (lloydia serotina), a species of flora endemic to Wales. It is also called the 'Snowdon lily' (cf. WELSH LILY).

**'Welsh Mountain wool':** Wool of WELSH MOUNTAIN SHEEP (A.M. Jones 1927:31). Often called simply WELSH WOOL.

**Welsh Mozart:** Magda writes that 'William Aubrey Williams, or by bardic title, Gwilym Gwent (1834-91) became known as the 'Mozart' of Pennsylvania's Wyoming Valley' (1986). Much of his music was composed on pit props and trams in the mines.

**Welsh Mr and Mrs:** The programme 'Siôn a Siân' which was based on the English version 'Mr and Mrs', testing couples to see how well they knew each other. 'Shôn a Shân' was also the barometre with the little man (Shôn) coming out on wet days and Shân on dry days (D. Parry-Jones 1952:106-7).

**Welsh mug:** A Welsh souvenir item which was a drinking mug with a WELSH LEEK design above the words 'Welsh mug' and a little hole at the bottom (a leak). See WELSH JOKE.

**Welsh mule:** Mixture of a blue faced Leicester and Welsh Mountain breeds. Also called 'Grey Face' or 'WELSH GREY FACE'. Mixtures are also experimented with WELSH MOUNTAIN, Beulah, Brecknock Hill, Cheviot and Hardy Speckle Face ewe. cf. WELSH HALFBRED.

**Welsh Mule Society:** Formed 1979.

**Welshmun:** Hum. name for a WELSHMAN, since in S. Walian speech, the word 'mun' is often interpolated.

**Welsh Musical Instruments, Queen of:** As the WELSH TRIPLE HARP is described (Yr Enfys, Winter 1996/97,3,9).

**Welsh Mussolini:** Darryl Jones writes 'If anyone were to have fulfilled W. Ambrose Bebb's desire for a "Welsh Mussolini", it would have been Saunders Lewis' (Planet 120:102). cf. WELSH GANDHI, WELSH HIPPY.

**Welsh mutations** (treigladau): This grammatical term refers to the change of the initial consonant of words in some circumstances eg. the word 'head' (pen) changes thus: 'ei ben e' (his head) – soft mutation – meddal; fy mhen i (my head) – nasal – trwynol and ei phen hi (her head) – llais – aspirant mutation.

**Welsh mutton:** (Ox.) Mutton from WELSH SHEEP. Sikes wrote that the Welsh sheep were 'the only beasts which will eat the grass that grows in the fairy rings . . . hence the superiority of Welsh mutton' (1880:109). cf. WELSH HAM, WELSH MOUNTAIN.

**'Welsh Mutton Hams':** A Victorian recipe of WELSH MUTTON, rubbed with treacle, thyme, marjoram and bay leaves, boiled and then hung up (Freeman 1996:137-8).

**Welsh N:** Often the WELSH NOT (qv.) had the words 'Welsh N.' or W.N. engraved on it.

**Welsh Nägeliapfel:** Common misspelling of Welsch Nägeliapfel, a Swiss apple variety also called 'Citron d'Hiver' or 'Winterzitrone' yellow to brown with red flush. cf. WELSH BEAUTY, WELSH PIPPIN etc.

**Welsh-named:** With a Welsh name. Eg. Carpenter and Prichard, alluding to Lady Charlotte Guest's translation of the 'Mabinogion' (1838), point out that the work was dedicated 'to the Welsh-named Ivor and Merthyr, two of her ten children' (1984:327).

**Welsh Naples:** Piehler wrote Llandudno is the 'Naples of the North' (1935:207). According to Frank Barrett 'Llandudno is 20 times better than grotty old Naples'. ('A View of Wales: Wales Tourist Board 1997 Holiday Magazine', p.31). See WELSH BIARRITZ, WELSH BLACKPOOL.

**Welsh Narrow Gauge Railway,** The: Title of book by J.D.C.A. Prideaux (pub. David and Charles) referring to the special type of railway in Wales.

**Welsh Nash:** WELSH NATIONALIST. See, for example, WELSH NASH WAY. cf. WELSH GNAT, WELSH NAT.

**'Welsh Nash Way',** The: The section of the dual carriageway from Cardiff to Abercynon, so called as it was petitioned for by Plaid Cymru, the WELSH PARTY (qv.) (see Gwynfor Evans 1992:111). cf. WELSH ROAD, WELSH WAY.

**Welsh Nat:** Like WELSH GNAT and WELSH NASH a nickname for WELSH NATIONALISTS.

**'Welsh National',** The: The Race at the Chepstow Racecourse on the Saturday before Christmas. cf. WELSH DERBY.

**Welsh National Anthem** (Yr Anthem Genedlaethol Cymru): The famous 'Mae hen wlad fy nhadau . . . ' (The Old Land of my Fathers . . . ), the words for which were written by Evans Jones and the music by his son in 1856. It has been adopted by other Celtic nations: In Breton 'Bro Gozh ma Zadou' and in Cornish 'Bro Goth agan tasow'. cf. WELSH NATIONAL ANTHEM, 2ND, WELSH RUGBY ANTHEM.

**Welsh National Anthem, The 2nd:** Ar hyd y nos (All Through the Night). cf. WELSH NATIONAL ANTHEM, WELSH RUGBY ANTHEM.

**Welsh National Assembly:** How the WELSH ASSEMBLY will be called after the Yes vote.

**Welsh National Costume:** As the WELSH COSTUME is sometimes called (eg. J. Lewis 1994-95:32).

**Welsh National Day** (Gŵyl Dewi Sant, Gŵyl Ddewi, Gŵyl Mabsant): March 1st, St David's Day. Many WELSH PEOPLE believe that a day off work should be granted. On this day a WELSH DAFFODIL or WELSH LEEK is worn. Before the Reformation it was a great religious celebration. Many WELSH NATIONALISTS believe that Wales should also celebrate a Llywelyn Day (11th Dec. anniversary of the death of Llywelyn ap Gruffydd at Cilmeri, 1282) and a Glyndŵr Day (16th Sept. when Owain Glyndŵr was proclaimed Prince of Wales at Glyndyfrdwy, 1400). See WELSH PATRON SAINT.

**'Welsh national drink':** Metheglin (even though WELSHMEN drink more beer). Many great WELSHMEN eg. Richard Burton (see THE WELSHMAN'S WELSHMAN) and Dylan Thomas (see the WELSH WIZARD) liked to drink. In the film 'Elizabeth Taylor' (1995) while filming 'Julius Caesar', Liz says 'You're not still drunk are you?', Richard Burton replies 'No, but I'm still Welsh, love – it's the same thing'. cf. WELSH DRUG, WELSH HOGSWASH, WELSH WINE.

**Welsh National Eisteddfod:** See WELSH EISTEDDFOD.

**Welsh National Flag** (Y Faner Gymraeg): The Red WELSH DRAGON or WELSH RED DRAGON on a green and white background.

**'Welsh national food':** WELSH RABBIT. See also WELSHCAKES, WELSH CAVIARE.

**Welsh National Garden:** David Jones describes Ebbw Vale as 'the only Welsh National Garden' (1992:21).

**Welsh National Ground:** So Cardiff Arms Park is dubbed (eg. by Moreton 1989:IGW:258).

**Welsh National Gymanfa Ganu:** Held by the WNGGA (Welsh National Gymanfa Ganu Association Inc.) in America for chapel-goers.

**Welsh Nationalism, The Apostle of:** So Lloyd George was called because of his early work in Cymru Fydd. Most WELSH NATIONALISTS would find this epithet inapt. See WELSH CAESAR AUGUSTUS, WELSH WIZARD.

**Welsh Nationalist:** A supporter of WELSH NATIONALISM, as seen in the creation of a WELSH ASSEMBLY and total independence from England. Unlike, many Irish Nationalists, WELSH NATIONALISTS give priority to the position of the WELSH LANGUAGE. Most WELSH NATIONALISTS would vote for the WELSH PARTY. See WELSH NATIONALIST PARTY.

**Welsh Nationalist – Green Alliance:** The co-operation between Plaid Cymru and The Green Party who have several common goals such as protecting Welsh heritage and the Welsh environment etc.

**Welsh Nationalist Party** (Plaid Genedlaethol Cymru): As Plaid Cymru was first known in 1925. Since W.W.2 and under the presidency of Gwynfor Evans the party grew considerably. As opposed to certain violent fascist kinds of nationalists, the policy of the Welsh Nationalist Party has always been 'cenedlaetholdeb' di-drais/di-dreisedd' (non-violent nationalism) and 'cymdeithasiaeth' (co-operative socialism).

**Welsh Nationalists' Way:** See WELSH NASH WAY.

**Welsh National League:** (See I.G.W. 111.)

**Welsh National Party:** Alternative term sometimes preferred to the WELSH NATIONALIST PARTY (eg. G. Evans 1988:352).

**Welsh National Sheepdog Trials:** In August at Dolgellau, Gwynedd.

**Welsh National Society** (Y Gymdeithas Genedlaethol Gymreig): Popularly called 'Y Tair G' or The 3 G's (from its initials in Welsh). Formed in 1922 by Lewis Valentine, Moses Griffith et al. an early WELSH NATIONALIST society which later merged with other groups to farm the WELSH NATIONALIST PARTY.

**'Welsh National Sport',** The: So rugby is called. See WELSH CAP, WELSH GOLDEN ERA. cf. WELSH CRICKET, WELSH HOCKEY, WELSH RELIGION.

**Welsh National Symbol:** See WELSH NATIONAL EMBLEM: WELSH DAFFODIL, WELSH DRAGON, WELSH LEEK.

**'Welsh National Territory':** As opposed to modern Wales, the larger area of 'Welsh National Territory' (a term used by the WELSH REPUBLICANS – see Gwer. 1996:178-9) includes large areas on the English side of the WELSH BORDER. These areas were part of Wales in C13th eg. the Oswestry Salient, passing through WELSHAMPTON, Ellesmere etc, The Chirburg Salient, The Clun Salient and west and south Herefordshire. Many Welsh people would like to see this land reincorporated into Wales.

**Welsh National War Memorial:** Unveiled by Prince of Wales, Cardiff, 1928.

**Welsh Nationhood:** The being of the WELSH NATION.

**Welsh Nats:** See WELSH NATIONALISTS. cf. WELSH GNATS, WELSH NASH.

**'Welsh Neanderthal Man':** Sara Erskine in a review of Heini Gruffydd's *Welsh is Fun* describes the book 'as a record of what preoccupied 1971 Welsh Neanderthal man – sex, rugby, beer, sex' (Planet 7:87, Aug./Sept. 1971).

**'Welsh Neo-classical Movement':** As Dafydd Johnston calls the influence of Goronwy Owen in C18th (1994:61).

**Welsh Neo-Classicists:** cf. WELSH HUMANISTS.

**Welsh nephew:** See WELSH NIECE, WELSH UNCLE.

**Welshness** (Cymreictod, Cymreigrwydd): The quality of being WELSH cf. anti-Welshness, as in Carol Trosset's *Welshness Performed: Welsh Concepts of Person and Society* (University of Arizon, 1993). See WELSH-WATCHING.

**Welsh Nessie:** The WELSH WATER MONSTER (qv.) or afanc.

**Welsh Newport** (Casnewydd): As opposed to the Newport in the Isle of Wight and the one in America etc. Yet confusingly there is also a second 'Welsh Newport' east of Fishguard (called Trefdraeth in Welsh). In Roderick's book, *Welsh Newport* refers to the aspects of Newport, Gwent that are Welsh (1994).

**Welsh Newton:** Place in Herefordshire.

**Welsh New Year:** 13th January according to The Old Calendar, Dydd Calan and still observed for some folk customs (Freeman uses phrase 1996:275).

**Welsh niece:** First cousin. The WELSH LANGUAGE is rich in terms for cousin: cefnder (male cousin), cyfnither (female), cyfyrder (2nd), ceifn (3rd), gorcheifn (4th) and gorchaw (5th). cf. WELSH COUSIN, WELSH UNCLE.

**'Welsh Niggers':** Despite the offensive word 'niggers', the term is not intended to offend. Arfon Jones, for instance, entitles his article about the black-anti-Apartheid demonstrators, and WELSH NATIONALISTS sharing joint rally 28.6.86 in Cardiff, *Nigars Cymraeg* (see Tudur ed. 1989:207). Y Niggers Gymraeg was a neologism by Rhodri Williams. He wrote in 1983 'Remember the WELSH-SPEAKING niggers'. In the film 'Proud Valley' (1940) when someone objected to going down the mine with black Paul Robeson he was told that 'at the end of the shift, Robeson's face would be no blacker than his own' (quoted by Richards 1993:13). There are many famous Welsh black people such as Shirley Bassey. Metaphorically WELSH PEOPLE have often been treated like 'niggers' in their own country. Not to be confused with WELSH BLACKS.

**Welsh night** (Noson Gymraeg): eg. in Vancouver WELSH SOCIETY each month. There are many forms of 'Welsh nights' with traditional entertainment: eg. noson lawen (merry night) cf. Breton-fest noz, hwyrnos (Welsh Night banquet – joio in S. Wales): noson goffi (coffee evening), noson werin (folk night), noswaith bilo/pilnos (peeling night), noswaith weu (knitting evening), noson cyflaith (toffee-making evening), noson bluo (feathering night) and noson ffarwelio (send off party on night before someone's departure – see Fynes-Clinton 1913:Vol.1, 129).

**Welsh Nightingale:** Singer Edith Wynne (1842-97), eisteddfod soloist who won fame in U.S.A. cf. The Cornish Nightingale – Fanny Moody of Redruth, The Swedish Nightingale Jenny Lind (1820-87) (the term 'Swedish nightingale' like the 'Irish nightingale' [Macafee 1996:235] refers to the hedge warbler or wood lark). Newgate nightingale was a gaolbird, the Fen/Cambridge/Dutch nightingale is a frog (cf. Nicholas Frog represents the Dutch as John Bull does the English; Froglander was a U.S. name for Dutchman – R.D. 1314). The Nightingale of the Holy Mountain (see WELSH HOLY MOUNTAIN) was Panteleimon Kartsonas (d.1992). Apart from Edith Wynne, Welsh poets have had the epithet nightingale (eos): eg. Eos Ceirig, Eos Eyns, Eos Gwynfa/y Mynydd and the lamented Siôn Eos. On similar lines to the Dutch Nightingale is the Arizona nightingale or Western nightingale (a donkey) (Clark 1996:248). The 'Gower Nightingale' is Phil Tanner (Sain Catalogue 1997-1998:p.37). cf. WELSH REGGAE, KING OF.

**Welsh Night of the Long Knives:** By allusion the German episode (30th June, 1934) or the Röhm Purge when Hitler killed all rivals. Borrow refers to Hengist's murder of Welsh/British chieftains as 'the treachery of the long knives' (1862. ch.Lii) (in Welsh 'Brad y Cyllyll Hirion'). The Welsh were all slaughtered at a banquet by the Saxons. History repeated itself at Abergavenny Castle 1177 when William de Braose (Ogre of Abergavenny) the WELSH MARCHER LORD similarly killed the unarmed men of Seisyll ap Dyfnwal again at a banquet. cf. The 'Black Dinner' in Scotland 1440 where William 6th Earl of Douglas and his brother were murdered at the table of Sir William Crichton and James II in Edinburgh Castle.

**Welshnik:** Hum. name for a WELSHMAN. cf. beatnik, kibbutznik.

**Welsh-Norman:** 1) That which pertains to both Wales and the Normans, eg. G. Evan's phrase 'Welsh-Norman struggle' (1974:191). 2) One of mixed Welsh and Norman parentage eg. Giraldus Cambrensis.

**Welsh North:** 1) So the 'Old North' is sometimes called (eg. by Ellis 1991:3) and ruled in the C5th-6th by the Gwŷr y Gogledd in Cumbria (related etymologically to 'Cymru). 2) As WELSH PEMBROKESHIRE is sometimes termed (eg. D.W. James, NWR 30:55) as it is in the north of the old shire.

**Welsh Not** (Y 'Not' Cymraeg): This was a piece of wood usually bearing the initial W.N. which was worn round the neck of a child who spoke Welsh in school. The child would pass it on to another child he caught speaking Welsh and the child wearing it at the end of the day would be beaten. A child so punished was termed a 'corryn' and other names for the Welsh Not were WELSH KNOT, WELSH LUMP, WELSH NOTE, WELSH STICK and Last Not. By entension other terms have been coined like 'fib not' (Mark Jenkins NWR 30:75) and 'Dialect Not' (referring to suppression of Anglo-Welsh Literature in favour of English (Reeves NWR 20:1, 1993). Alun Williams uses the term 'English-Not' to refer to monoglot English children having to learn Welsh (quoted by N. Jones 1993:145). Exact parallels of the Welsh Not are seen in Ireland with the 'bata scóir' or 'tally-skick' (which Parry-Jones calls the 'Irish Not' 1964:150). The 'maide crochaidh' (stick on a card) for Gaelic-speaking children, in Brittany the 'vache' (buoc'h ie. cow), sabot (clog) or simbol (symbole) (see Renouard, 1992:319). In Malta the 'accipe' was used, in the Basque country the 'eraztun' (ring) or 'txartela' (card). In the Russian Black Sea area Pontian Greek children wore the 'tabel'. See WELSH LANGUAGE, WELSHLESS and following entries:

**Welsh-not:** Hyphenated form of WELSH NOT (qv.) used eg. by N. Jones (1993:123,146).

**Welsh Note:** Another name for the WELSH NOT.

**Welsh Noting:** Punishment by use of the WELSH NOT.

**'Welsh Not mentality':** Concept to describe the complex of one who is ashamed of his native tongue (H.T. Edwards 1990:23).

**'Welsh Not Policy':** As Ned Thomas dubs the anti-Welsh policy in schools (1973:115).

**Welsh Nots:** Llewellyn's spelling of WELSH NOT (1974:39). The final -s is strange for the singular form (particularly since there was only one in the classroom which would be passed around).

**Welsh Not syndrome:** The syndrome of being ashamed of one's language and ceasing to use it because of persecution. cf.

WELSH NOT MENTALITY.

**Welsh-notted:** (of a child) punished by having the WELSH NOT tied round the neck.

**Welsh Nuadha Airgedlámh:** Dixon-Kennedy observes 'Lludd Llaw Ereint' is 'the Welsh equivalent of Nuadha Airgedlámh' (1997:197). Both names in Welsh and Irish mean 'Silver Hand'.

**Welsh Nursery Movement** (Mudiad Ysgolion Feithrin): Also called Welsh Nursery School Movement f.1971. The movement also tries to improve the Welsh of WELSHLESS parents with groups such as 'cylch ti a fi' and 'cylchoedd mam a'i phlentyn'. Parallel organisations can be seen in other Celtic counties: Diwan in Brittany (f.1977), Dalleth in Cornwall (f.1979) and Manx Chied Chesmad (first step) etc.

**Welsh nut:** The walnut. In Wiltshire still called 'welchnut'. Hendrickson writes 'Even the ancient word walnut is a kind of slur on the Welsh – it comes from the Anglo-Saxon "Wealhhnutu", "the foreign or Welsh nut",' (1983:220). In Devon called the French nut (cf. French bean which is WELSH BEAN qv.).

**Welsho:** The -o suffix is a hum. form (see Alwyn ap Huw 1995:11) usually mocking in tone. cf. 'boyo' which as Todd says 'is common both as a term of address and reference, and is sometimes negative in tone' (McArthur ed. 1992:1107).

**Welsh oak dresser** (Dreser dderw): See WELSH DRESSER.

**Welsh oatcakes:** Freeman tells us that 'Welsh oatcakes traditionally were huge – "big as dinner plates" ' (1984:22), 10 inches or more rolled by hand and put on iron shelves of oven with a 'crafell' (wooden paddle).

**Welsh oatmeal chests** (cistiau styfflog): Long oak chests used for grain etc. but also household linen.

**Welshocentric:** Centred on Wales cf. Anglocentric, Eurocentric.

**Welsh Office** (Y Swyddfa Gymreig): Est. 1964 and housed in Cathays Park, Cardiff, The Welsh Office subsidises Welsh publishing, employs civil servants and releases statistics of

Welsh school, homes, accidents and hospitals.

**Welsh-office:** (adj.) That which is organised, subsidised, employed etc. by the WELSH OFFICE.

**Welsh Office Civil Service Jargon:** See WELSH OFFICE SPEAK (qv.).

**Welsh Office Minister:** Who is minister of the Welsh Office. cf. WELSH OFFICER.

**Welsh Office Speak** (W-O-Speak): Term used by Merfyn Williams (NWR 29:106, Summer 1995).

**Welsh Office Undersecretary:** Assistant of the WELSH SECRETARY.

**Welsh Officer:** An employee of the WELSH OFFICE. cf. WELSH OFFICE MINISTER.

**Welshoid:** (Hum.) A being/thing in Welsh form cf. Creoloid etc.

**Welsh oilstone:** (Encycl. Brit.) Idwal or 'Welsh oilstone' is a hone 'used for small articles', used for whetting or sharpening tools.

**Welsholatry:** Worship of/admiration for that which is Welsh.

**'Welsh Old Boys' Network':** So Isaacs and Law call the Taffia, (1994:416). See WELSH MAFFIA.

**Welsh 'O' Level:** See WELSH GCSE.

**Welshology:** The study of Welsh culture and things about Wales and the WELSH. cf. WELSH ETHNOLOGY.

**Welshomania:** Mania for that which is Welsh. cf. Anglomania, Celtomania (Stephens ed. 1986:545), Francomania, Gallomania etc.

**Welshomaniac:** One who 'suffers from' WELSHOMANIA.

**Welsh omelet:** Omelet made with WELSH ONION, ham, a little butter and salt and pepper. cf. WELSH PANCAKE.

**'Welsh on':** Eleri Carrog quotes script from Emmerdale Farm

'I'd never do a Welsh on you' (Planet 83:115, Oct./Nov. 1990). In fact, as well as 'to do a Welsh on' one can also say 'to Welsh on'.

**Welsh one-night cottage** (Tŷ/tyddyn unnos): Tiny squatter's hut built overnight which builder could own if he managed to light fire in it before daybreak. In Turkish the 'gecekondu' is the same.

**Welsh onion:** The chibol, cibol. Interestingly there is a whole entry for the Welsh onion in 'Japan: An Illustrated Encyclopaedia' (Kodansha, Vol.2:1697, 1993) according to which there are three Japanese varieties of 'negi' (Welsh onion): hakushú, shimonita, akanegi.

**Welshood:** See WELSHHOOD.

**Welshophile:** A friend of the Welsh. cf. WELSH-LOVING. David Lloyd uses the term 'Cymriphiles' (Planet 116:79).

**Welshophilia:** Love of the Welsh. Similarly Peter Morgan coins the term 'Celtophilia' (Planet 125:32, 1997).

**Welshophobe:** One who hates (literally 'fears') the Welsh. cf. Russophobe, Turcophobe etc.

**Welshophobia:** Fear/Hatred of the Welsh. cf. H.T. Edward's phrase 'Celtophobia' (NWR 34:18-20).

**Welshophone:** A WELSH-SPEAKER. cf. Anglophone, Francophone.

**Welsh Order of Merit, Leeke's:** Ranking system for sportsmen.

**'Welsh Organisers'** (Y Trefnyddion Cymraeg): The WELSH PRESBYTERIANS (Humphreys 1983:158).

**Welsh Orifice:** Making a pun on the WELSH OFFICE, Dylan Iorwerth writes 'The Welsh Orifice is a black hole' (Planet 102:110, Dec.1993/Jan.1994).

**Welsh-originated:** That which originates from Wales eg. 'Welsh-originated programmes' (G. Evans 1991:62).

**Welshosity:** That which is Welsh. Coined by analogy with Welsh curiosity.

**'Welsh Otherworld':** As Green calls Annwn (1992:172). Ellis calls it the 'Cymric Otherworld' (1992:25), Funk and Wagnalls the 'Brythonic Otherworld' and Matthews and Matthew the 'British Underworld (1988:24). In Welsh mythology it is the abode of Arawn (in Mabinogion) and Gwynn ap Nudd (in legends). See WELSH FAIRY KING, WELSH GOD OF THE UNDERWORLD, WELSH HELL HOUNDS.

**Welshousity:** See WELSHOSITY.

**Welsh Overseas** (Y Cymry Tramor): See WELSH EXILES SOCIETY.

**Welsh Ovid:** See WELSH HORACE.

**Welsh-owned:** Owned by Wales or by a Welsh company.

**Welsh Oz:** See WELSH PRIVATE EYE.

**Welsh Pacifist Movement:** A Welsh nationalist society of conscientious objectors at the time of W.W.2. and the secretary of whom was Gwynfor Evans. Stephens thus translates the Welsh 'Heddychwyr Cymru' twice (1996:52) and also provides the alternative translation of 'The Peacemakers of Wales' (ibid.:41).

**Welsh Paddy:** A Hiberno-Welshman, ie. one of Welsh and Irish parentage.

**Welsh 'Padrones':** Term Fishlock uses to describe the bosses in the WELSH ATHENS (NWR 22:73, 1993). cf. WELSH CAUDILLOS.

**'Welsh Page':** As page in 'Western Mail' dedicated to Welsh news since 1968 is often called (Planet 123:28, 1997).

**'Welsh Pagliacci':** By A. Gene Hillstrom, Parallax Press. Title of biographical work. (The word is Italian for 'clowns').

**'Welsh Pale':** See WELSH HEARTLAND.

**'Welsh pan/pot loaves:** Type of Welsh bread (Lady Llanover 1867:473).

**Welsh pancake** (Crempog Cymreig): A.T. Ellis (ed. 1989:38) quotes an old recipe of Countess Murphy made with batter from flour, sugar, baking powder, bicarbonate of soda, milk, whey, jam and butter but no eggs.

**Welsh Park Sheep, Black:** A breed of WELSH SHEEP (see Williams-Davies 1981:29). cf. WELSH HALBRED, WELSH MOUNTAIN, WELSH MULE.

**Welsh Parliament** (Senedd i Gymru): The WELSH ASSEMBLY. The last real one was held by Owain Glyndŵr at Machynlleth.

**Welsh Parliament House** (Senedd-dŷ Owain Glyndŵr). The actual building in Machynlleth where Owain Glyndŵr held his WELSH PARLIAMENT.

**Welsh Parliament Petition:** 250,000 signatures presented to House of Commons in 1956.

**'Welsh Parliamentary Party':** Phrase used by John Osmond (Planet 109:109, Feb./March 1995).

**Welsh Parliamentary Committee:** Est. 1907 to deal with committee stage of bills concerned just with Wales.

**Welsh Parnell:** Or the Parnell of Wales, epithet of Thomas Edward Ellis (1859-99), politician and supporter of WELSH HOME RULE.

**'Welsh parrot':** J. Geraint Jenkins writes 'The cry of a bird, known locally as the "Welsh parrot", that screeches the words "Dim byd, dim byd" (nothing, nothing) also signifies that the particular fishing season when it appears will be without a catch, particularly if that bird flies across the river and over the fishing . . . ' (1992:182). It is uncertain which bird this is – perh. cf. the 'sea parrot' which is the Tenby name for a puffin? (Shillings 1970:161). This is also supported by The Ulster English meaning where 'Welsh Parrot' means a puffin (also called in Ulster Ailsa cock (parrot) (Macafee) 1996:382). See WELSH AMBASSADOR, WELSH CORPSE BIRD, WELSH FALCONER, WELSH RED KITE.

**Welsh parsley:** Strong hemp and by extension 'Welsh parsley' refers to 'the hangman's noose' (Green 1996:298). cf. Chinese parsley-coriander leaf.

**Welsh Part-Bred:** Hyphenated form of WELSH PART BRED.

**Welsh Part Bred,** (large): (Of a pony) which according to the WELSH PART BRED REGISTER is a pony with not less than 25% Registered WELSH BLOOD and seen in terms like Welsh Part Bred colt, filly or gelding etc. Not to be confused with WELSH HALFBRED (qv.) cf. WELSH COB, WELSH MOUNTAIN PONY, WELSH PONY.

**Welsh Part-Bred Cob:** A pony with at least 25% WELSH COB blood.

**Welsh Part-Bred Horse:** The largest part-bred in Wales.

**Welsh Part-Bred Horse Group:** Set up in 1987 under the auspices of the WELSH PONY AND COB SOCIETY.

**Welsh Part Bred Register:** See WELSH PART BRED.

**Welsh Partridge:** A dry fly used for fishing (M. Morgan 1996:97). See WELSHMAN'S BUTTON, WELSH SHRIMP FLY.

**Welsh Party** (Plaid Cymru): See WELSH NATIONALIST PARTY.

**Welsh Passport:** Unlike the Nansea passport (issued through League of Nations for stateless persons), the Welsh Passport is basically a souvenir item with a WELSH DRAGON symbol and the details inside in WELSH and English (not French and English). The passport does look realistic and I have heard of three Celtic cousins going through a few E.E.C. countries with just Cornish passports!

**Welsh Patagonian Colony:** As G. Evans refers to the WELSH COLONY (qv.) (1988:260).

**Welsh Patagonians:** The WELSH PEOPLE who live in the WELSH COLONY of Patagonia, Argentina. They first arrived with Michael D. Jones in 1865 and now speak WELSH and Spanish.

**Welsh Patriot:** Perhaps the most famous WELSH PONY OF

COB TYPE (foaled 1939) and owned by Mr A.L. Williams. His son was WELSH ECHO (foaled 1944). Also the name of the Welsh Labour Party's newspaper 'Y Gwladgarwr Cymreig' in early years.

**Welsh patriotism** (gwladoldeb Cymreig): Patriotism for Wales, as opposed to Britain. The term connotes support for Welsh causes, loyalty to the WELSH NATIONALIST PARTY and preference for the WELSH LANGUAGE etc.

**Welsh Patron Saint** (Dewi Sant) C6th: St David son of Non and Sant was grandson of King of Ceredigion. There are many legends about him eg. when he resisted the temptation of Boia wife of the Irish chieftain who sent him naked girls (all other monks yielded). He is supposed to have ordered his soldiers to wear the WELSH LEEK in battle. The most famous legend is when a white dove perched onto his shoulder while he was preaching. In the Middle Ages his shrine was an important place for pilgrimages. Many WELSH PEOPLE wear the WELSH DAFFODIL on his day. His biography was written by Rhigyfarch and he was canonised by Pope Callixtus in 1120. See WELSH APOSTLE, WELSH LOVERS, PATRON SAINT OF, WELSH NATIONAL DAY.

**'Welsh Patron Saint of Love':** As Hutton refers to Dwynwen (1996:148). See WELSH ST VALENTINE.

**'Welsh Patronymics':** Phrase used to describe the Welsh naming system (Emrys Jones, Yr Enfys, Autumn 1996:5). The most common feature is ab/ap (son of) before father's first name (surnames were a later non-Welsh form of naming) eg. Dafydd ap Gwilym (see WELSH HORACE). The less common feminine form of 'ab'/'ap', that is 'ferch' (daughter), has also been used. Patronymics are also used in many Slavic nations eg. Russia.

**Welsh pearl:** A counterfeit pearl, flattish and blackish. cf. WELSH DIAMOND. See WELSH PEARL MUSSEL.

**Welsh Pearl Mussel:** As Carson Ritchie refers to the vanishing genus of freshwater mussel, margariti fera margaritifera Linn

(Planet 78:76, Dec/Jan. 1989-90). He writes 'The Welsh themselves . . . called them krigin diliw, shells brought to Wales by Noah's flood'. See WELSH PEARL.

**Welsh peasant costume/dress:** A synonym of WELSH COSTUME (qv.), Lady Charlotte Guest wrote in 1838 'I went to the Cambrian Ball in my Welsh peasant's dress.'

**Welsh pedigree, as long as a:** See WELSH GENEALOGY.

**Welsh Pee Wee Herman:** Siân Hughes in a review of Rhys Davies' *Ram With Red Horns* writes 'Here Rambo meets the Welsh answer to Pee Wee Herman' (NWR 39:88, 1997-98).

**Welsh Pembroke corgi:** See WELSH CORGI. Also called WELSH PEMBROKESHIRE CORGI.

**Welsh Pembrokeshire:** As opposed to the WELSH 'LITTLE ENGLAND'. The northern WELSHRY of Pembrokeshire (now part of Dyfed) with a WELSH-SPEAKING population, seperated from WELSHLESS English speakers by an imaginary border known as the Landsker. cf. WELSH CORRIDOR, WELSH GAELTACHT, WELSH HEARTLAND.

**Welsh Pembrokeshire corgi:** Another name for the WELSH PEMBROKE CORGI. See WELSH CORGI.

**Welsh penny wedding:** A tradition not confined to Wales, but also seen in Scotland, parts of England etc. whereby guests help pay for expenses. This is called 'talu'r pwyth' (paying a debt) ie. – repaying the contribution they were given at their own wedding or 'dechrau byw' (starting life) etc. cf. WELSH HORSE WEDDING.

**Welsh Penrhyn:** Actually the full name is Penrhyn-coch (red promontory) and sometimes the Welsh is prefixed to distinguish it from the Penrhyns in Cornwall and in Cumbria (Lands of the Western WELSH and OLD WELSH respectively). There is also a Penrhyn in the Cook Islands.

**Welshpeople:** Can be written as one word. cf. WELSHMAN, WELSHWOMAN.

**Welshperson:** Can be written as one word or hyphenated.

**Welsh phantom funeral** (toili): Premonition of a funeral which will occur cf. Irish crócharnaid. One of the names for the WELSH HELL HOUNDS (qv.) is 'cŵn toili'. cf. WELSH BANSHEE etc.

**Welsh Pharaohs:** In 1880 William Price of Llantrisant said 'You the coal-owners are the Welsh Pharaohs who think you can suck the life-blood of the colliers for ever . . . Remember the oppression of the Pharaohs did not last for ever, and neither will the oppression of the blood-sucking pharaohs of Wales' (quoted by M. Stephens, ed. 1992:55). cf. WELSH MOSES.

**'Welsh phoenix':** Cardiff Bay – the development of which by Peter Walker, Secretary of State for Wales is described by Kevin Williams as 'enabling the Welsh phoenix to rise from the ashes' (Planet 121:8, 1997).

**Welsh pibgorn:** Ellis prefixes the 'Welsh' to the old instrument 'pibgorn' (1991:48) as does Woodhouse (1994:25). Funk & Wagnalls write of the pibgorn 'known in its primitive form in Wales as a section of the shinbone of a sheep with a bell of cow's horn' (p.869). It had seven holes. cf. WELSH BAGPIPES, WELSH DOUBLE CHANTER, WELSH COUBLE HORNPIPE, WELSH HARP, WELSH HORNPIPE, 'WELSH VIOLIN'.

**Welsh pidgin:** Type of pidgin of half-Welsh and half-English (see WELSH SHIPRIS). Not to be confused with 'Pidgin Welsh' or 'Mongrel Welsh' as WELSHLESS anglicised WELSHPEOPLE are sometimes called.

**Welsh pig:** 1) The Welsh pig, WELSH WHITE or simply WELSH (qv.) is an old breed of lop-eared pig native to Wales. 2) The map of Wales (due to its resemblance to pig's head). In Welsh mythology there was Henwen the pig that produced Cath Palug (the cat monster) and the monster boar Twrch Trwyth (cf. Ir. Torc Triath). According to Funk and Wagnalls 'The modern Welsh are said to believe that the pig appears on Halloween, and during an eclipse people imitate the grunting of pigs' (p.869). Ifan ab Owen Edwards (1895-1970) was called 'a stubborn Welsh pig' when he wrote home from the W.W.1 trenches in Welsh (G. Evans 1988:332).

**Welsh pipes:** See WELSH BAGPIPES. See also WELSH PIBGORN.

**Welsh Pippin:** Also called Marmalade Pippin and Althorpe Pippin. Like the WELSH BEAUTY (qv.) it is an old variety of apple which is now lost. It was recorded in 1818 and 1884. It was revived not in Wales but Derbyshire (see Smith 1971). cf. WELSH'S SPITZENBERG.

**Welsh plaid:** See WELSH KILT, WELSH TARTAN.

**Welsh plain:** WELSH FLANNEL.

**Welsh plough** (aradr Gymreig): A distinct wooden form of plough from Wales.

**'Welsh Poet',** The: John Davies (1565?-1618) from Hereford who 'was known during his lifetime as "The Welsh poet" . . . ' (Garlick 1970:33, Stephens ed.1986:131).

**Welsh Poet and Priest:** R.S. Thomas (b.1913). From title of his book by M.J.J. van Buuren *Waiting: The Religious Poetry of Ronald Stuart Thomas, Welsh Poet and Priest* (1994). cf. WELSH PREACHER-POET.

**Welsh Poet of the Modern Mind, The First:** As Saunders Lewis called hymnwriter Pantycelyn (William Williams 1717-91) (quoted by G. Evans 1974:336-7).

**Welsh Political Prisoners' Defence Committee:** Formed following the arrest of some WELSH SOCIALIST REPUBLICAN MOVEMENT members for arson. Their first meeting was at Tŷ'r Cymry, Cardiff. cf. WELSH CAMPAIGN FOR CIVIL AND POLITICAL LIBERTIES. See WELSH SUMMER HOUSES.

**Welsh Politics, The Crucible of:** As Prof. K.O. Morgan describes Merthyr Tydfil (quoted by Balsom 1996:88).

**Welsh Politics, Sisyphus of:** So Dylan Iorwerth refers to Welsh

Republican Movement (Planet 60:114, Dec./Jan. 1986-7). In Greek mythology Zeus punished Sisyphus by making the latter roll a large stone up to the top of a hill which would then roll back down again and Sisyphus would have to repeat this.

**Welsh Polo:** Sian Llewellyn (1974:27) refers to Cnapan/Knappan – a game in which 'a leather ball sewn and stuffed was pursued with sticks by horsemen – a sort of polo'. cf. WELSH HOCKEY, WELSH WRESTLING.

**'Welsh polypody':** (Vulgare cambricum) a type of oak fern (Sanders, p.341).

**Welsh Polymath:** Edward Lhuyd (1660?-1709) distinguished both as a scientist (botanist, chemist, lithographer) and a philologist (a pioneer of research in the Cornish language etc.). See WELSH AISLE.

**Welsh poney:** Older spelling of WELSH PONY.

**Welsh ponies A, B and C:** First three section of WELSH MOUNTAIN PONY, WELSH PONY and WELSH PONY OF COB TYPE, not including the slightly larger and hardier WELSH COB.

**Welsh pony** (merlod): Breed from the Welsh Mountains, used for children and pony-trecking up to 12.2 hands (and often smaller). Head is clean cut with alert small ears. See WELSH PONY SECTION B. cf. WELSH COB, WELSH KEFFEL.

**Welsh Pony and Cob Society** (Cymdeithas y Merlod a'r Cobiau Cymreig): Society founded 1901 for promoting and breeding the four types of native Welsh ponies: WELSH MOUNTAIN PONY, WELSH PONY, WELSH PONY OF COB TYPE, WELSH COB. Its journal also gives information about WELSH PART BREDS (qv.).

**Welsh Pony and Cob Vereniging Show:** Held at Hetern, Holland (see CSJ. 1991., pp.176-9). cf. Welsh Pony Stamboek, Holland. The WELSH PONY is very popular abroad, especially amongst Dutch horselovers.

**Welsh Pony Cob Type:** See WELSH PONY OF COB TYPE

SECTION C.

**Welsh Pony of Cob Type:** See WELSH PONY OF COB TYPE SECTION C.

**Welsh Pony of Cob Type Section C:** As the WELSH PONY AND COB SOCIETY brochure reads 'The WELSH PONY OF COB TYPE is the stronger counterpart of the WELSH PONY but with cob blood'. In competitions its category must not exceed 13.2 hh (137 cm).

**Welsh Pony Section B:** Larger than the WELSH MOUNTAIN PONY (SECTION A. QV.), the WELSH PONY should not exceed 13.2 hh (137 cm) and is used mainly for riding.

**Welshpool** (Y Trallwng): Originally called just Pool but the 'Welsh' was added to distinguish it from Poole in Dorset.

**Welsh Pool:** A form of WELSHPOOL (Adrian Room, from McArthur 1992:1109).

**Welshpool Coracle:** A variation of the WELSH CORACLE (qv.) from WELSHPOOL. (See J. Geraint Jenkins 1988:122-4).

**Welshpool Railway:** An old fashioned mountain railway network in Wales. Correctly it is Welshpool and Llanfair Railway.

**Welsh poppy** (meconopsis cambrica): In Welsh pabi coch yr ŷd or llygad y bwgan (eye of the ghost). A yellow poppy native to Wales and S.W. England and Ireland.

**Welsh Portofino:** As Portmeirion is called as its design was inspired by Portofino in Italy. See WELSH XANADU.

**Welsh Portrait Gallery:** A proposed gallery that would be a Welsh version of the London equivalent. Advocated by Gordon Stuart according to Peter Stead (Planet 118:17, Aug./Sept. 1996).

**Welsh postage stamps:** See WELSH STAMPS.

**'Welsh potato basket':** As John describes the round, bowl-shaped 'gwyntell' basket made of willow/hazel rods and laths and without a handle (1976:12).

**Welsh potboard dresser:** A type of WELSH DRESSER from Montgomeryshire, mid C18th – open at the bottom for the purpose of storing pots and larger crockery (the smaller plates being displayed on top). cf. WELSH CUPBOARD-BASE DRESSER.

**Welsh Potosi:** Don Dale-Jones writes 'It was in 1690 that Sir Corbery Pryse discovered silver in his Gogerthan estate at Eskairhir. The deposits were optimistically named "The Welsh Potosi" '. (NWR 11:59, 1990-91). Potosi was a Bolivian silver mine. cf. WELSH GOLD.

**Welsh pot-shell:** Like a garden snail but lattice furrowed and waved with yellow like Welsh potware.

**Welsh pound:** Apart from coins and tokens made by individual companies in Wales, there are two WELSH POUND COINS, one bearing the emblem of the WELSH LEEK and around the edge the words 'Pleidiol wyf i'm gwlad' (taken from the WELSH NATIONAL ANTHEM). The other has a WELSH DRAGON. cf. WELSH STAMPS.

**Welsh pound coin:** See WELSH POUND.

**Welsh praise-poetry:** Poetry in praise of a lord or lady (who patronised the poet). See, for example, Stephens ed. (1986:480). The Gogynfeirdd composed both 'marwnad' (praise of the dead) and 'moliant' (praise of the living). Another now obs. term was 'gwawdlef' – poetry or song of praise.

**Welsh preacher-poet:** A phenomenon of literary figure in Wales: a poet who is a minister. As J. Lewis writes 'The Welsh preacher-poet continues to thrive and is often to be found chaired or crowned at the National Eisteddfod of Wales . . . ' (1989:65). cf. WELSH-ANGLICAN, WELSH POET AND PRIEST.

**Welsh Presbyterians:** Or Presbyterians of Wales. Also called Calvinistic Methodists. WELSH CALVINISTIC METHODS and WELSH METHODISTS etc. As opposed to Welsh Baptists etc. who are just Baptists that are Welsh-speaking, the WELSH

PRESBYTERIANS in their doctrine and organisation are a separate denomination, by virtue of 1927 Act of Parliament. Once called 'jumpers' because of their excitement at meetings. Most of the chapel conduct services in Wales. There are two 'cymdeithasfa' (Synods) for N. and S. Wales. They also have 'cwrdd dosbarth' or district meeting at which individual chapels are grouped and 'cwrdd misol' presbytery into which the 'cwrdd dosbarth' is grouped into larger units. The 'Cymanfa Gyffredinol' is the Annual General Assembly at which the moderator is elected. Each individual chapel holds a 'seiat' – fellowship meeting and 'sasiwn' – quarterly association. Outside Wales, chapels are to be found in Liverpool, London and Manchester, as well as overseas missions. See WELSH REVIVAL.

**Welsh Press', 'Father of the:** William Rees (Gwilym Hiraethog, 1802-83) (May 1994:331).

**'Welsh prestige ladder':** A sociological term coined by Emmett (1964). There is an English ladder which is separate and a Welsh one 'based on local ethnic activities', prestige being given to those who display most WELSHNESS (Trosset also uses the term 1993:82-3).

**Welsh Priest:** 'Sir, there is a fray to be fought, between Sir Hugh the Welch Priest, and Cains the French doctor' (Shakespeare, *Merry Wives of Windsor*, 1958, 2, i).

**Welsh Prince:** Prince of Wales (Tywysog Cymru). This is an ambiguous term. For many WELSHMEN the Welsh prince is historically not the son/heir of the English throne, but a title that belonged to rulers of the Welsh, the last of which was Llywellyn. cf. WELSH HIGH KING, WELSH PRINCEDOM, WELSH PRINCIPALITY, WELSH SUB-KINGS.

**Welsh Prince, The Last:** Llywelyn (Ein Olaf) or Y 'Llyw Olaf', Llywelyn ap Gruffudd (c.1225-82).

**Welsh princedoms:** The territory of an old WELSH PRINCE, and was part of Wales. See WELSH DIVISION.

**Welsh princelings:** Miles' term for the lesser WELSH PRINCES (1969:34).

**Welsh Principality:** Or The Principality of Wales. Many WELSHPEOPLE are still sensitive to the word principality (tywysogaeth) just as Cornish Nationalists are to the word 'Duchy' as the term connotes the domain of a WELSH PRINCE who was a vassal of the English King.

**Welsh 'Private Eye':** Tripp and Stephens write of the periodical 'Lol' that it 'could be described as the Welsh 'Private Eye' or 'Oz' if the satire was a bit more wicked and the nudes more shocking' (Planet 9:60, Dec. 1971/Jan. 1972). cf. WELSH PUNCH, WELSH TIT BITS.

**Welsh Problem, The:** As the English have often referred the cause of WELSH NATIONALISM (eg. Hearne 1977:17).

**'Welsh process':** Process in which copper ore is smelted and then changed to metallic copper by alternative roasting and smelting in reverberatores, superseded by Bessemer converting. cf. WELSH METHOD.

**Welsh-produced:** Produced in Wales or by Welsh companies.

**'Welsh Progency Competition':** The 'best group of three progency within a particular section by the same sire or out of the same mare nine times' (W. Davies 1993:54-6). In relation to the WELSH PONY and WELSH COB.

**Welshproof:** (Hum.) Able to withstand the Welsh cf. bullet proof, shockproof.

**Welsh Proms:** Welsh equivalent of the Proms, eg. in July 1991 at St David's Hall, Cardiff.

**Welsh Prophecy, Antichrist of:** As T.B. Edwards refers to Harri Tudur/Henry Tudor (VII) who betrayed Welshmen who had regarded him as 'mab darogan' (son of prophecy) that would deliver them (The Celtic Pen, Vol.1, Issue 3, Spring 1994:21).

**Welsh Prose-Writers, The Doyen of:** As M. Stephens describes Anglo-Welsh (but WELSH-SPEAKING) novelist Glyn Jones

(1905-95) (BWA, No.40, p.16, June 95).

**Welsh Protomartyr:** William Seward, the first WELSH METHODIST martyr who, like Stephen The Protomartyr (first martyr) was stoned to death (while preaching at Hay-on-Wye, Powys, 1742).

**Welsh Pudding** (Pwdin Cymreig): A winter recipe similar to Bakewell pudding (Freeman 1988:74).

**Welshpudlians:** Natives of WELSHPOOL. cf. Liverpudlians.

**Welsh Punch** (Y Punch Cymraeg): The Welsh version of the Punch Magazine with most woodcuts drawn by Ellis Owen Elis. cf. WELSH PRIVATE EYE, WELSH TIT BITS.

**Welsh Pygmalion:** M. Wynn Thomas says of Emlyn William's book '*The Corn is Green* is a collier's rags to educational riches story: a Welsh Pygmalion' (NWR 9:10, 1990).

**Welsh 'Pyramids':** The two large towers on the Menai Suspension Bridge (completed 1825) which Telford called 'Pyramids'.

**Welsh Quakers** (Y Crynwyr Cymreig): Also called the WELSH FRIENDS, the Welsh Quakers went to Pennsylvania in 1682. See WELSH TRACT.

**Welsh Quangos** (Cwangos): An abbreviation of Quasi – autonomous national governmental organisations and refers to the English-authorised organisations in Wales. Wales, due to her many Quangos has sometimes been called Quangoland.

**Welsh Quarter:** 1) Like a 'Jewish quarter', a Welsh area or neighbourhood of a town/city, especially in Cardiff, eg. 'Cardiff's "Welsh Quarter", Pontcanna' (Bulsom ed. 1996:64). By contrast, Emrys Jones writes that 'The Welsh in London were well-scattered with no locality which could be called a Welsh quarter' (Yr Enfys, Autumn 1996:6). 2) Gwen Davies writes: 'Standing above the industrial estate on the A48 at Briton Ferry, Sister Margaret Clare pointed out to me what appeared to be a "Welsh Quarter " containing some forty families. But considering how the sites gentle scripture teacher had also described the ancestors of the "WELSH TRAVELLERS" as dispossessed Dan-y-Graig peasants, a remarkable number of them turned out to have Irish names and crucifixes in their caravans' (Planet 60:61, Dec./Jan. 1986-7). WELSH GAELTACHT, WELSH HEARTLAND, WELSHRY.

**Welsh quarterbred:** The offspring of a WELSH HALFBRED.

**Welsh Question:** Analogous with the Irish Question and referring to matters such as WELSH HOME RULE etc.

**Welsh Question Day:** As the WELSH DAY (qv.) is sometimes called (eg. by Stephens in index 1996:257; yet also WELSH QUESTIONS DAY ibid:195).

**'Welsh question-time':** (Stephens 1996:182). See WELSH QUESTION DAY.

**Welsh Questions Day:** See WELSH QUESTION DAY.

**Welsh quilting** (cwiltion Cymreig): Type of quilting in Wales done by a cwiltreg (female quilt-maker).

**Welsh Quisling:** G.H. Jenkins refers to one ashamed of his own language as a 'Welsh quisling' (from Vidkun Quisling, Norwegian wartime traitor, executed 1945). At the WELSH DEBATE (24.11.49) a woman said to the Labour minister, James Griffiths, 'You are a Quisling, Jim Griffiths. Go back to Wales. We want a WELSH REPUBLIC' (quoted by Gwer. 1996:15).

**Welsh 'R':** In Welsh the letter 'r' is always rhotic (pronounced), unlike, for example, the 'r' in the English 'arm'. cf. WELSH 'RH'.

**Welsh rabbit** (caws pobi, enllyn caws, tocyn Cymro): Dish of cheese (with milk and eggs mixed) toasted on bread and popularly translated 'toasted cheese'. It is also called 'Scotch rabbit' (DHS). cf. Bombay duck (dried fish), Scotch woodcock (toast and anchovy paste), German duck (half sheep's head boiled with onions – no relation to WELSH DRAKE), Irish horse (salted meat), Cornish duck (pilchard) and Manx goose (herring) etc. According to legend St Peter could only lure them out of Heaven by shouting Welsh rabbit (caws pobi) whereupon they all left. The dish is sometimes called WELSH RAREBIT. Apart from Scotch rabbit (identical to 'Welsh rabbit', DHS), 'There are also American rabbit (with whisked egg whites), English rabbit (with red wine), Irish rabbit (with onions, gherkins, vinegar and herbs), and Yorkshire rabbit (topped with bacon and a poached egg)' (Ayto 1994:376). The Welsh Rabbit is also a dance. cf. WELSH RABBITS, SOCIETY OF.

**Welsh rabbit pudding** (Pwdin caws pobi): A pudding version of WELSH RABBIT (qv.) soaked in milk and baked in oven.

**Welsh Rabbits, Society of:** Club founded by C.E. Mathews, Adam-Reilly and Morshead at Pen y Gwryd, 1870. The purpose of the society was to explore Snowdonia in winter. See WELSH ALPS, WELSH HIGHLANDS, WELSH MATTERHORN, WELSH SUB-ALPS, WELSH 3,000S, WELSH TIGER.

**'Welsh rabbit stew'** (Potes cwningen Cymru): Recipe with young rabbit, butter, bacon rashers, mushrooms, onion, carrot, potatoes, flour, stock (Sian Llewellyn 1974:71).

**'Welsh Radicalism':** A distinct political philosophy. Jackson writes 'as opposed to English Liberalism and giving direction to the new WELSH NATIONALISM' (1889:42).

**Welsh rag:** (Ox.) Slates in patent slating. cf. WELSH LAY, WELSH LUMP.

**Welsh ram:** Traditionally rams of WELSH MOUNTAIN were given the best ewes whereas 'less good to the Suffolks' (M.C. Harris 1980: 18). Sometimes an unlucky ram since the WELSH MOUNTAIN EWE is often mated with Leicester ram for a WELSH HALFBRED.

**Welsh rarebit:** A synonym of WELSH RABBIT. See also WELSH RAREBITS. In 1994 Lyn Gardiner brought out a book *Welsh Rarer Bits*. As Howells tells us 'A Buck Rarebit is . . . served with a poached egg on top' (p.14). Here the allusion to a 'buck' seems to indicate preference for WELSH RABBIT rather than rarebit.

**Welsh Rarebit, Cream** (Hufengaws wedi pobi): WELSH RABBIT made with cheese and cream (S. Llewellyn 1974:84).

**Welsh Rarebit, St John's:** Variation of the Welsh recipe from St John's Restaurant, London including stout, mustard and chilli ('Oxfam Fairworld Cookbook', p.16).

**Welsh Rarebit Hotels:** The Welsh Gold Collection of 39 hotels and inns, mostly small and privately owned.

**Welsh Rarebits:** A chain/consortium of accommodation – hotels etc. Also *Welsh Rarebits – Jokes from Wales* was the title of a little book by Harry H. Hughes (Cyhoeddiadau Mei).

**Welsh raw wool:** Raw, untreated WELSH WOOL from WELSH SHEEP (J.G. Jenkins 1985:14).

**Welsh-reading:** By analogy with WELSH-SPEAKING, Owen refers to the 'Welsh-reading public' (1991:119), ie. those able to read or who habitually read Welsh.

**Welsh Rebel Hero:** So Owain Glyndŵr is described in Cadw's *On The Wales Heritage Trail* map. See WELSH WARRIOR-STATESMAN.

**Welsh Rebellion:** 1) The WELSH REVOLT (qv.) 2) As Harri Webb calls The Rebecca Riots (1839) (Gwer. 1996:97).

**Welsh Red Dragon Flag:** See WELSH FLAG.

**Welsh red kite** (barcut): A bird not unique to Wales but it is associated with Wales as it is the only region of Britain where the bird is found. It is also found in N. Africa and Gibraltar (in 1996 Gibraltar issue a series of four stamps featuring this bird). cf. WELSH AMBASSADOR, WELSH CORPSE BIRD, WELSH DRAKE, WELSH FALCONER, WELSH PARROT.

**'Welsh Reel'** (Dawns Werin Llanofer): Traditional dance kept alive by Lady Llanover and today still performed in schools in Llanover on St David's Day (GFWI, 1994:93). cf. WELSH JIG, WELSH MORRIS.

**Welsh Red and White, National:** The National Welsh buses.

**Welsh Red Indians:** As the WELSH INDIANS (qv.) are

sometimes called (see Humphreys 1983:71, 109-13 and G. Evans 1988:202).

**Welsh Referendum:** The 'Refferendwm' took place on St David's Day, 1979 in both Wales and Scotland. Only 58% of WELSH electorate voted of which 243,048 voted for devolution and 956,330 against. See WELSH VETO. In September 1997 Wales voted for (by just 6,000 odd votes).

**'Welsh regicide:** As Miles calls Welsh Parliamentarian Col. John Jones of Merioneth, brother-in-law of Oliver Cromwell who signed Charles I's death warrant (1969:128).

**'Welsh Region':** As Trosset calls 'Y Fro Gymraeg' (1993:9). See WELSH GAELTACHT, WELSH HEARTLAND.

**Welsh Reggae, The King of:** According to the ACEN catalogue (1995-1997) – Geraint Jarman a'r Cynganeddwr Cyfrol 1 (Sain). cf. WELSH NIGHTINGALE.

**Welsh Regiment** (Y Gatrawd Gymreig): Usually spelt Welch Regiment. The 4th, 5th and 24th battalions captured Jerusalem from the Turks in 1917.

**Welsh Regiment Chapel:** A post-war feature of Llandaff Cathedral.

**Welsh-related:** (adj.) Related to Wales or to that which is Welsh eg. as used by David Lloyd (Planet 116:78).

**'Welsh Religion':** As rugger is called (Moreton 1989 IGW:257). See WELSH CAP, WELSH GOLDEN ERA, WELSH NATIONAL SPORT, WELSH RUGBY ANTHEM.

**Welsh Renaissance:** The phrase refers to the renaissance/rebirth of Welsh literature (see, for example, NWR 25:77, Summer 1994) David Rees mentions 'a group of Welsh Renaissance men of letters' from Tudor times. The term 'Welsh Renaissance' can also be applied to Iolo Morganwg's renaissance of Gorsedd and forging medieval poems etc. (Jackson 1989:39). Indeed recently John Harris speaks of a 'Welsh literary renaissance' (NWR 11:28, 1990-91). Jackson also refers to the C18th London Welsh societies as 'a mini-

Renaissance' (ibid). In the world of folk culture and art, B.S. John talks of the 1960's and 1970's as a 'Welsh Craft Renaissance' (1976:3). cf. WELSH CLASSICS, WELSH HUMANISTS.

**Welsh Representative Bureau:** In Brussels office where Wales is represented in Europe. See WELSH EUROPEAN.

**Welsh Republic:** For WELSH NATIONALISTS, an independent Wales.

**Welsh Republic, Workers Army of the** (Wawr): The Welsh meaning of the initials is 'dawn'. WAWR was an extremist political party in the late 1960's and early 1970's and many of their members were arrested for the arson campaign. The party is no relation to the Welsh women's association of the same name. cf. WELSH CAMPAIGN FOR CIVIL AND POLITICAL LIBERTIES.

**Welsh Republicanism:** Political ideology of the WELSH REPUBLICAN MOVEMENT (Gwer. 1996:32).

**Welsh Republican Manifesto:** Manifesto of the WELSH REPUBLICAN PARTY (Gwer. 1996:25-6).

**Welsh Republican Movement** (Mudiad Gweriniaethol Cymru) Phrase refers to the brand of socialist WELSH NATIONALISM as in title of Donald Gregory's *Young Republicans: "Gweriniaethwr" (or Welsh Republican Movement)* (Carreg Gwalch).

**Welsh Republican Party:** See WELSH REPUBLICAN MOVEMENT. (Gwer. 1996:16).

**Welsh Revival** (Y Diwygiad): 1) The religious Revivals in WELSH METHODISM eg. 1750, 1859 and 1904. cf. WELSH REVIVALIST, THE GREAT. 2) The recent revival of the WELSH LANGUAGE over the last three decades with organised WELSH CLASSES, promotion of books, WELSH FOURTH CHANNEL etc.

**'Welsh returners':** As N. Jones refers to those WELSH EXILES who go back to Wales after a long absence, as opposed to the incomers (1993:134).

**Welsh Revivalist, The Great:** Evan Roberts (1878-1951). The epithet derives from D.M. Phillips' work 'Evan Roberts, The Great Welsh Revivalist and his work' (1923). He was an evangelist and leader of the 1904 WELSH REVIVAL.

**Welsh Revolt:** 1) Led by Madog ap Llywelyn (1294-5) against tax on arable goods, conscription of Welsh soldiers for Gascony campaign and the Statute of Rhuddlan (1284). It was crushed by Edward I. 2) So Owain Glyndŵr's rebellion is sometimes called (1403). cf. WELSH REBELLION.

**Welsh Revolution:** Apart from the WELSH REVOLT (qv.) Hearne uses this term for the struggle of modern WELSH NATIONALISM (1982).

**Welsh 'Rh':** A strongly aspirate 'r' for which the phonetic symbol is r. In the WELSH ALPHABET it comes after 'r'. Hence in a Welsh dictionary, as opposed to the English order, the entry for 'rŵan' (now) comes before 'Rhagfyr' (December). In Coelbren it is represented by a separate letter Y (WELSH R is Y).

**Welsh Rialto:** Caerleon. The epithet derives from Trevelyan who had called Caerleon 'The Rialto of all Britain'.

**'Welsh Ribbon':** A large ribbon made by Linda Bevan-Smith and Heulwen Jones of the Wellington WELSH SOCIETY. It is hanging in the Galeria of the New Zealand Parliament building with motifs of the WELSH DRAGON, WELSH DAFFODIL, WELSH HARP, WELSH LEEK, castle and WELSHLADIES (see Yr Enfys, Summer 1996 p.17).

**Welsh Ride, The:** An old WELSH DROVERS' route in Hampshire now a grassy path with gorse and heather (M.C. Harris 1980:11). There is also a Welsh Ride near Gloucester which is also called the WELSH DRIVE (Moelwyn Williams *A South Wales Landscape*, p.102). cf. WELSH ROAD.

**Welshrie:** Like WELSHRYE an old spelling of WELSHRY (qv.)

**Welsh Riviera:** Thompson wrote 'On this stretch of Welsh 'Riviera' from Llandudno to Prestatyn and the wide mouth of the Dee there is a place for everyone' (1937:244). cf. The south coast of Cornwall which is dubbed the Cornish Riviera (the 'Cornish Riviera' also referred to the Express train following that route from and to London). cf. WELSH BIARRITZ, WELSH BLACKPOOL, WELSH MARGATE.

**'Welsh road':** Damp lane green with ferns. cf. WELSH LANE.

**Welsh Road:** 1) Elias says that WELSH DROVERS used 'yr enwog "Welsh Road" drwy Coleshill, Kenilworth, Southam, Culworth . . . Buckingham, Leighton Buzard, Dunstable, Watford a Barnet', (1987:36); 2) Another WELSH DROVERS' route used to carry salt from Cheshire to Northamptonshire (Grimes 1991:264). cf. WELSHMAN'S FIELDS, WELSH RIDE, WELSH WAY.

**Welsh Robin Hood:** Twm Siôn Cati (c.1530-1609), Welsh folk hero. He is likened to Robin Hood by many writers notably Meyrick (1822) and Nicholson etc. His adventures are believed to be based on the life of Thomas Jones of Tregaron. In America there is an organisation called 'Twm Siôn Cati Welsh American Legal Defence and Education Fund'. In parts of South Wales, Jackie Kent (fl.1400) is 'The Robin Hood of the banks of the Wye' (T.A. Davies 1937:41). The Danish Robin Hood is Marsk Stig. The Scots Robin Hood is Rob Roy (see WELSH ROB ROY) and the Turkish Robin Hood is the outlaw Koroglu. The Polish Robin Hood is Janosik. See WELSH DICK TURPIN.

**Welsh Rob Roy:** Another epithet for Twm Siôn Cati (see the WELSH ROBIN HOOD) from the title of Samuel Rush Meyrick's *The Welsh Rob Roy* (1823).

**Welsh Rock and Roll, The Bad Boys of:** So Anhrefn are dubbed (Sain Catalogue 1997-1998, p.125).

**Welsh rock cinquefoil** (pontentilla rupestris): The 'Welsh' is not always prefixed and the (Welsh) rock cinquefoil is a flower endemic to Wales. cf. WELSH POPPY.

**Welsh Roehampton:** May writes that in 1918 'The Prince of Wales Orthopaedic Hospital was opened in Cardiff – "The Welsh Roehampton" '.(1994:118).

**Welsh Rolls:** Records (Encycl. Brit.).

**Welsh Romances, The Three** (Y Tair Rhamant): A term often used for Iarlles y Ffynnon (Owain), Geraint and Peredur (found in *The White Book of Rhydderch* and *The Red Book of Hergest*).

**Welsh Romanies:** See WELSH GYPSIES.

**Welsh Romany Dynasty, the Founder of:** So John Roberts, the WELSH GYPSY HARPIST (qv.) is called by Robin Huw Bowen (*English Dance and Song* Vol.56, No.4, Winter 1994, p.21).

**Welsh Room:** 1) As Rosser tells us 'The Welsh Room is a little known room off Westminster Hall. It had been known as such for many years, since only Welsh MPs ever used it' (1987:51). 2) Gwynfor Evans may have used his house as an equivalent since he tells us that when his aunt died, 'I made her bedroom into a "Welsh room" ' (Stephens, trans. 1996:10). 3) A proposed room at the National Museum of Wales (Planet 126:94, 1997).

**Welsh-rooted:** (Ox.) with the roots lying in Wales.

**Welsh round house** (tŷ crwn): Or WELSH CIRCULAR HOUSE, a unique type of Welsh building, circular in shape and medieval. cf. WELSH LONG-HOUSE.

**Welsh Round Table:** By analogy to King Arthur's Round Table, Humphreys writes of 'One of the knights of Lloyd George's Welsh Round Table, the barrister and author Llewelyn Williams, his erstwhile bosom friend' (1983:209).

**Welsh Rudolph Valentino:** Ivor Novello (David Ivor Davies, 1893-1951) so called because of his classical profile and good looks. He could also compose, and write plays.

**Welsh Rugby, The Headquarters of:** So Cardiff Arms Park is called (eg. Yr Enfys, Summer 1995, p.9)

**Welsh Rugby Anthem:** The popular 'Sosban Fach' or 'Little Saucepan'. Moreton also calls this song 'the "national anthem" of Llanelli'. The hymns 'Cwm Rhondda' (Guide me O Thou Great Jehovah) and 'Calon Lân' ar also sung. cf. WELSH NATIONAL ANTHEM.

**Welsh Rugby, Grand Old Man of:** As G. Smith calls Rhys Gabe, one of the great stars who led Wales to victory over New Zealand in 1905 (1993:41).

**'Welsh Rugby's First Superstar':** As Roderick calls 'The Immortal Arthur Gould' (fl. 1890s) (1994:56).

**'Welsh Rule':** The rule to speak Welsh and conduct proceedings in Welsh at the eisteddfod (Stephens ed. 1986:423).

**Welsh-ruled:** Ruled by Wales.

**Welsh-run:** Run or organised by Wales.

**Welsh Run, The:** A place in Pennsylvania. cf. WELSH TRACT.

**Welsh runt:** (No relation to the WELSH PIG). The Welsh runt is the name for WELSH CATTLE bought by English graziers in the Midland counties. See WELSH BLACK CATTLE.

**Welshry** (brodoraeth): 'A now rare term for Welsh people, a part of Wales where Welsh is used, an area where Welsh people live and Welsh descent' (McArthur ed. 1992:1109-10). A plural connotation, eg. G. Evans writes 'The "Welshry" were up in the hills, where they had mainatined their traditional Welsh way of life' (1994:172).

**Welshrye:** G. Owen wrote of Pembrokeshire (1603) 'This shere is taken to be devided into two partes, that is to the Englishrie and Welshrye'.

**Welsh St Valentine:** St Dwynwen (C5th) who is also known as the 'Patron Saint of WELSH LOVERS'. Or 'The St Valentine of Wales' (Jeffrey, p.67). In love with Maelon, she asked God to stop her feelings (as her father Brychan Brycheiniog had betrothed her to another prince). God granted her three wishes: to help Maelon, that she would never love again wish to be married and to answer requests made by her on behalf of those truly in love. On her feast day (January 25th) some celebrate it as the WELSH ST VALENTINE'S DAY and send 'falendein' (pl. ffolantau) – valentines or 'cardiau serch santes Dwynwen' (St Dwynwen cards for lovers.) See WELSH PATRON SAINT.

**'Welsh Sabbath-school':** William Williams wrote in 1872 that: 'The Welsh Sabbath-school . . . is a very different affair from anything called by that name which they can find in England. It is not merely an institution of teachers and children merely, but a meeting where the great bulk of the congregation . . . assemble together to instruct one another in Divine Things' (quoted by Jones and Davies 1986:73). cf. WELSH CIRCULATING SCHOOLS.

**Welsh saga poetry:** A category of old long saga-type poems.

**Welsh Saint of Animals and Nature:** As Melangell is called – to whom Plethyn sing song in album *Byw a Bod.* There is also The Mudiad 'Gwyrdd' Cymreig. – Cymdeithas Melangell, a type of Welsh ecological group (Sain Catalogue 1997-1998, p.39).

**'Welsh Saints':** Really the name should apply to the old Welsh saints eg. WELSH PATRON SAINT, WELSH PATRON SAINT OF LOVERS (or Patron Saint of WELSH LOVERS) and the WELSH SAINT OF ANIMALS AND NATURE etc. It is also how Welsh Mormons called themselves (Planet 73:42, Feb./March 1989). cf. WELSH MORMON EXODUS.

**Welsh salmon:** Just as the Manx salmon is not salmon but bollan wrasse (bollan or braddan) so the 'Welsh salmon' is not salmon (eog) but the 'sewin' or WELSH SEATROUT (salmo truta). It is fished with the WELSH CORACLE. If under 2 lb it is called a 'shinglin', if 2-3 lb a 'twlpyn' and if 3-20 lb a 'gwencyn'.

**Welsh salt box:** Listed in Millers Antiques Price Guide 1998.

**Welsh Salt Duck** (Hwyad Hallt Cymreig): Duck prepared with onions, bay leaf, parsley and peppercorns (Freeman 1988:79).

**Welsh sandwich** (brechdan ddwbl): Oatcake and bread eaten as a sandwich. Single 'brechdan' is buttered bread. cf. Manx 'breaghdan' (buttered cake). A 'Cornish sandwich' is jam and clotted cream on a scone (Waller 1994:41).

**Welsh Saturnalia:** W.J. Gruffydd said in 1931 'St David's Day . . . the Saturnalia which releases us all from of patriotism and its responsibilities for a whole year' (quoted and translated by M. Stephens, ed.1992:87-8).

**Welsh Saudi Arabia:** Sinclair describes Tiger Bay as 'The Saudi Arabia of the nineteenth century' (1993:1). See WELSH CHECKPOINT CHARLIE, WELSH SOHO.

**Welsh Savonarola:** Sir J.E. Lloyd wrote of the prior of the Cistercian monastery of Llantarnam, John ap Hywel, that he was: 'a strenuous preacher of repentance and patriotic self-devotion, whom Bower compares to Jonah, stern reprover of the sins of Nineveh, but who may more fittingly be regarded as a Welsh Savonarola warning his countrymen that the success which had hitherto followed their aims would be forfeited by a continuance of their evil living' (1931:97). (Savonarola (1452-98) was the notable figure of the popular government of Florence (1490s) whose supporters were called 'piagnoni' (weepers) because of their penitential practices).

**'Welsh scarlet':** (The 'red' 'pump y dore'). Red was originally made from the cockles, especially at coast, as opposed to cochineal etc. (now used just for confectionary).

**Welsh Scholars** (Y Cymreigyddion): f.1794 as a debating society among London WELSHMEN and interested in social reform. Other famous societies of 'Welsh Scholars' were The Cymreigyddion y Carw Coch (founded by William Williams at the Stag Inn) and Cymreigyddion y Fenni (f.1833 in Abergavenny).

**Welsh scones:** As Smeeth calls WELSH CAKES (1994:97).

**Welsh Scouse:** A Welsh Liverpudlian or Liverpudlian of Welsh extract. The word 'scouse' is by the way, related to the N. Walian dish 'lobscows'; (cawl in S. Wales). cf. WELSH CAPITAL.

**Welshs Creek:** Or Welchs Creek, a place name.

**Welsh Sea, (A little bit of) Lancashire beside a:** So Colwyn Bay is described (Piehler 1935:207). cf. WELSH MARGATE etc.

**Welsh sea trout:** See WELSH SALMON.

**Welsh second homes:** See WELSH SUMMER HOUSES.

**Welsh second National Anthem:** See WELSH NATIONAL ANTHEM 2ND.

**Welsh Secretary:** A government post in Wales. cf. WELSH AFFAIRS, MINISTER FOR, WELSH OFFICE.

**Welsh Section A Pony:** See WELSH MOUNTAIN PONY SECTION A.

**Welsh Select Committee:**

**'Welsh Senate':** Katie Gramich uses the term 'Welsh Senate' (Planet 114:78, Dec.1995/Jan.1996) (J. Hearne 1982:59) for WELSH ASSEMBLY or WELSH PARLIAMENT. cf. Welsh 'senedd'.

**Welsh Senedd:** As Richard Wyn Jones calls the concept of a WELSH PARLIAMENT (qv.) (Planet 118:69), Aug./Sept. 1996). 'Senedd' is the Welsh word for parliament and a cognate of senate.

**Welsh-set:** (Of a story etc.) set in Wales. Christopher Meredith uses word (NWR 13:31, 1991).

**Welsh settle:** Welsh version of the settle-long wooden seat with high back, usually of oak. cf. WELSH DRESSER.

**Welsh Settlement:** The settlement of the WELSH PATAGONIANS in Chubut Province. See WELSH COLONY.

**Welsh settlers:** Those who settled in Patagonia. See WELSH COLONY.

**Welsh Shadow Secretary:** See WELSH SECRETARY.

**Welsh Shaft:** Part of the Great Laxey Wheel in the Isle of Man.

**Welsh Shakespear:** See WELSH SHAKESPEARE.

**Welsh Shakespeare:** Thomas Edwards/Twm o'r Nant (1738-1810). Twm o'r Nant was the great author of interludes (metrical plays). Borrow calls him the 'Welsh Shakespeare'

(1862, Ch XIII) and he is also called the 'Cambrian Shakespeare'. Indeed for more 'connection' between Wales and Shakespeare see NWR 22:2 (Autumn 1993) and Tom Lloyd-Roberts 'Bard of Lleweni? Shakespeare's Welsh Connection' (NWR 23:11-18, Winter 1993-94). See WELSH CAPTAIN. According to Brewer The German Shakespeare was Kotzebue (1761-1819), The Spanish Shakespeare-Calderón fl. C17th. cf. WELSH BUNYAN, WELSH DEMOSTHENES, WELSH HORACE etc.

**Welsh shaman:** The 'dyn hysbys' or WELSH CONJUROR (qv.).

**Welsh shawl:** The shawl (or 'siôl') is an indispensable part of the WELSH COSTUME. See WELSH FASHION.

**Welsh Sheep:** See WELSH MOUNTAIN SHEEP.

**Welsh Sheep, (badger faced)** (Defaid Torddu): A mountain breed of sheep from Wales, so called because of dark face marking (like that of a badger). Williams-Davies says that 'The presence of badger-faced sheep in a flock was at one time regarded as being a sign of bad luck' (1981:30). A Society was formed in 1977 to protect and preserve the breed.

**Welsh Sheep Dog Trials, Royal:** At Aberystwyth.

**Welsh Sheepskins:** Hides of WELSH SHEEP (A.M. Jones 1927:88) which were sent to tanneries.

**'Welsh sheep strategy':** Huw Thomas uses this phrase in reference to the WELSH OFFICE'S Agricultural Department's policy to promote WELSH SHEEP ('The Western Mail: Country and Farming', Tuesday, 23 September, 1997, p.8).

**Welsh Sheeptacular:** The half hour performance of sheepshearing, sheephandling and sheepdogs at Glan Valley, Vision Centre, Rhyader (so billed in 'Mid Wales – Festival of the Countryside/Gŵyl Cefn Gwlad y Canolbarth', pub. Festival of the Countryside, Newton, 1991 p.44).

**Welsh Shell trumpet:** Trumpet made by cutting the apex of a conch shell-used by women in certain remote hill farms of N. Wales to call their husband. Around Bangor district it was called 'Krogan vu:yd' (Fynes-Clinton 1913:297).

**Welsh Shield:** Won by the Under 15 Welsh Schools Knockout Tournament in football (Yr Enfys, Winter 1996/97:18).

**Welsh shipris:** Or Sipris Welsh (Cymraeg Shipris). To 'Sharad Shipris' is to speak 'a mixture of English and Welsh' (Morris 1910:285). Such a language is also called 'bratiaith' or 'Cymraeg cerrig calch' and in N. Wales the word 'myngral' (ie. mongrel) was 'applied to one who cannot speak either Welsh or English correctly' (Fynes-Clinton 1913:381). The etymology of shipris 'siprys' is from the mixture of oats and barley (cf. 'canrhyg' is the mixture of rye and wheat). cf. WELSH ENGLISH, WELSHLESS.

**Welsh Shorthand:** A unique Welsh system of shorthand distinct from Pitman's and invented by Thomas Roberts as explained in his book *Stenographia* (The Greek word for 'Shorthand') in 1839.

**Welsh shot** (siot): 1) 'Picws mali' – the oatbread and buttermilk dish. 2) The custom of 'talu siot' (paying 'shot') referred to paying a contribution to help the bereaved family with funeral expenses.

**Welsh shovel:** J. Williams writes that the Welsh 'rhaw' 'is not strictly speaking a shovel – it has a point, and a bent handle' (1973:114). Similarly the long-handled 'Cornish shovel' is also a distinct tool. cf. WELSH GLAIVE.

**Welsh Show, German National:** Annual show in Germany with WELSH PONIES (qv.). (See CSJ, 1991:173).

**Welsh Show, Royal** (Sioe Frenhinol Cymru): See WELSH AGRICULTURAL SHOW, ROYAL.

**Welsh Showground, Royal:** Builth Wells.

**'Welsh shrimp fly':** A special fly for fishing salmon (M. Morgan 1996:139-40). See WELSHMAN'S BUTTON, WELSH PARTRIDGE.

**Welsh side:** The Welsh side of the border: or the Welsh team in a sports match.

'Welsh Signatories': As the seventeen Welshmen who signed the American Declartaion of Independence are called.

Welsh silver mark: The Plumes (of Prince of Wales) as shown on some Aberystwyth coins. cf. WELSH GOLD.

Welsh sin eaters (Y Bwytawr Pechodau): Poor people who were offered food, especially bread and beer usually over the corpse as it was believed that they took the deceased person's sins away. cf. WELSH SOUL CAKES.

Welsh single harp (telyn unrhes): See WELSH HARP, WELSH TRIPLE HARP.

Welsh sing-song: The distinctive lilt or musical intonation that is characteristic of the Welsh accent so called by many eg. Thompson (1937:105). In extreme fervour and emotional excitement as in sermons of WELSH METHODIST ministers, the 'Welsh sing-song' can rise into a 'hwyl'.

Welsh single strung harp: Or WELSH SINGLE HARP. See WELSH HARP.

'Welsh Sinn Feiner': As Welsh political correspondent Llygad Llwchwr was called because of his nationalist sympathies. He wrote in August 1950 'there is a good spicy taste about being called a Welsh Sinn Feiner' (quoted by Gwer. 1996:35). The comparison is, of course, derived from The Irish Nationalist party Sinn Fein.

'Welsh sires': WELSH PONY and WELSH COB studs (Wynne Davies 1993:9,28). The term could also be applied to WELSH MOUNTAIN rams.

Welsh six-lobed daffodil: The WELSH DAFFODIL so called because of its hexagonal lobes.

Welsh Skimmington: So 'cwlstrin' or 'ceffyl pren' (wooden horse) is called. The custom refers to parading a person or his effigy in streets usually at night, usually for some kind of sexual immorality, especially adultery. The term 'ceffyl pren' corresponds with non-Welsh variations where the adulterer or remarried widow(er) is paraded on a horse. In Scotland the parallel custom is 'Riding The Stang'. The term 'Rough Music' is also found in parts of England, in Cornwall 'shallall', French 'charivari', Spanish 'esquellotada' and Basque 'tober(r)a'/ 'galarrotza'. The most common English term is Skimmington (hence the Welsh Skimmington).

**Welsh slate** (sleten, llechen): Welsh slate is from the Ordovician or Lower Silurian Age). It was used to gather cream from milk, for roofs, of course and the aquarium of London Zoo was built of Welsh slate. There is also a Welsh Slate Museum.

**'Welsh slate-quarrying novels':** As Dafydd Johnston calls a sub-genre of Welsh prose characterised by Caradog Prichards' *Un Nos Ola Leuad* (1961), and the works of Kate Roberts and T. Rowlands, (1994:109).

**Welsh 'S' Level:** An 'S' level in WELSH.

**'Welsh slogan', The:** Cymru am Byth (Wales for Ever) which corresponds with the Breton 'Breiz Atao' and psuedo-Irish 'Erin go brach' (ie. Eire go brath).

**Welsh-Smith:** A double-barrelled surname eg. C.U.P. authoress Susan Welsh-Smith. (In Welsh Smith is 'gof').

**Welsh smock:** See WELSH WOOLSMOCK.

**'Welsh snake stones'** (maen magl, glain y nadroedd): Polo-mint shaped stone used by the WELSH CONJUROR for magic. These were believed to be bubbles spat by snakes forming a circle and good luck. A potion made with a snake stone in was called 'dŵr y trochwyd'. cf. WELSH STAR SLIME.

**Welsh snuff:** (Ox.) Like Lundyfoot a 'high dried' snuff.

**'Welsh soap', The:** See the WELSH CORONATION STREET.

**Welsh Socialist Republican Movement** (WSRM): In Welsh 'Mudiad Gweriniaethol Sosialaidd Cymru'. Group that split away from the WELSH PARTY, Plaid Cymru. Their paper was 'Y Faner Goch' (The Red Flag). Always sympathetic to arsonists and explosions and the police identified them with WAWR (see WELSH REPUBLIC, WORKERS ARMY OF THE) who conducted arson campaign in late '60s and early '70s.

**Welsh Socialist Republican Party** (Plaid Gwerin Cymru): A short-lived political group that emerged in the 1960s (see Ellis 1985:94).

**Welsh Socialist Vanguard:** On 21:7:73 John Jenkins wrote a letter from prison alluding to several contemporary political groups, mentioning 'The sudden emergence of UNITED WELSH ACTION, Mudiad Werin Cymru, Welsh Socialist Vanguard, W.P.P.D.C. et al. with the Hosts of Rebecca, Free Wales, Y Gweriniaethwr and so on . . . ' (1981:72). These groups were extremist and short-lived.

**Welsh Societies, Union of:** A group which merged with the COMMITTEE TO SAFEGUARD CULTURE to form Undeb Cymru Fydd.

**Welsh Society, The Secret** (Y Gymdeithas Gymreig Gudd): A society formed by Harri Pritchard Jones (see NWR 22:50).

**'Welsh Sodom':** So Hughes and Evans describe the decadent town of Llys Helig which was destroyed by a flood (1986:55). As with Lot and the few survivors from Sodom, a few innocent people were rescued from Llys Helig. cf. WELSH ATLANTIS.

**Welsh Soho:** The Tiger Bay area of Cardiff has been so designated beacuse of its bars and clubs. See WELSH CHECKPOINT CHARLIE.

**Welsh Soldiers and 'White' Officers:** 'The term was coined by Welsh soldiers, who suspected that in the view of their 'superiors' they were little different to troops recruited in Africa or India' (quoted by Boyston Jones in the context of Lloyd George wanting a 'Welsh Army' – Link No.3/Welsh Monitor, Sept./Oct. 1995, 9, No.5). cf. 'WELSH NIGGERS'.

**Welsh Soldier-Poet:** Hedd Wyn (Ellis Humphrey Evans 1887-1917) poet whose 'awdl' (type of Welsh ode) entitled 'Yr Arwr' (The Hero) won posthumously the choir at Birkenhead – called 'Eisteddfod y Gadair Ddu' (The Eisteddfod of The Black Chair).

**Welsh sorrel** (Acetosa Cambro-Britanica montana): A wild

flowering plant found in Wales.

**Welsh 'soul cakes'** (cacen gŵyl y meirw, pice rhanna, cacennau enaid): Cakes eaten on behalf of the dead soul. In the past poor people would go a-souling (hel solad) or collecting food-cakes etc. Those who gave food to the poor would help the souls of their loved ones. cf. WELSH SIN EATERS.

**Welsh-sounding:** That which sounds Welsh (eg. D. Williams 1975:49).

**'Welsh Soup':** Violet Norman of Llanelli recounts 'there was always "cawl", The Welsh Soup' (quoted by Grenfell-Hill 1996:143). See WELSH BROTH.

**Welsh Spaniel** (Sbaniel Cymreig): A Welsh breed of Spaniel. The Spaniel is well-represented by Celtic breeds cf. Breton Spaniel (épagneul breton) and Irish Water Spaniel. See WELSH CORGI, WELSH FOXHOUNDS, WELSH HELLHOUNDS, WELSH SPRINGER SPANIEL, WELSH TERRIER.

**Welsh-Speaker:** One who speaks Welsh. Unlike the term WELSH MONOGLOT, the speaker's ability to speak English (or another language) is not ruled out.

**Welsh Speaker's Day:** See WELSH SPEAKING DAY.

**Welsh-Speaking:** (Adj.) Or more rarely 'Cymrophone', that which relates to speaking in Welsh. cf. WELSH-WRITING.

**'Welsh speaking budgie':** Palfrey and Roberts refer to an eisteddfod winner who was supposed to have been 'A Welsh speaking budgie from Rhyl' (1994:9).

**'Welsh-Speaking cow':** Harri Webb's phrase '3 acres and a Welsh-speaking cow' (1962) based on 1880's slogan and with reference to Plaid Cymru's economic policies. (Quoted by Stephens ed. 1992:132). cf. WELSH BLACK.

**Welsh Speaking Cowboys:** Robert Owen refers to these in review of Glyn Williams' *The Welsh in Patagonia* (Planet 89:89, Oct./Nov. 1991). See WELSH GAUCHOS. cf. WELSH-SPEAKING INDIANS.

**Welsh-Speaking Day** (Diwrnod Siarad Cymraeg): A day organised to give WELSH LEARNERS (particularly those living outside the WELSH HEARTLAND) an opportunity to meet with fellow-learners and native WELSH-SPEAKERS to practise their WELSH.

**'Welsh-speaking Doeg tribe':** As De Camp calls the Doeg tribe who, like the Mandans, have been called WELSH INDIANS. The Doeg tribe were supposed to have saved Morgan Jones in 1660 when he was about to be killed by the Tuscaroras as they understood him (see De Camp. 1970:124).

**Welsh-Speaking Evening:** An evening organised to give WELSH LEARNERS and WELSH SPEAKERS a chance to speak Welsh – as often organised by the Vancouver Welsh Society (see 'Yr Enfys' Spring/(Summer 1995:16).

**Welsh-Speaking Heartland:** As the WELSH HEARTLAND (qv.) is sometimes called (Hodgson 1983:62; A.W. Jones 'Contact Bulletin' Vol.10, No.2, Autumn 1993, p.2).

**'Welsh speaking incomers':** Frankenberg uses this term (1957:64) to distinguish non-local WELSH SPEAKERS from English speakers who migrate to the WELSH HEARTLAND.

**Welsh-speaking Indians:** See WELSH INDIANS.

**'Welsh-speaking Lesbian and Gay Community:** As CYLCH ('Circle') is called by Michael Nobbs (Planet 118:128, Aug./Sept. 1996).

**Welsh-speaking 'media yuppies':** Noragh Jones uses this term to refer to those 'whose values and life styles are not consistent with the traditional rural mores' (1993:136).

**'Welsh-Speaking pit':** A coal pit where the miners are/were WELSH-SPEAKING (phrase used by Janet Davies, Planet 113:37, Oct./Nov. 1995).

**Welsh-speaking Red Indians:** As G. Evans (1988:197) calls the WELSH INDIANS (qv.).

**'Welsh-speaking Sea':** With reference to Dylan Thomas'

Landscape (or rather seascape), (quoted by Ioan Bowen Rees, NWR 25:23, Summer 1994).

**Welsh-speaking Welshman** (Cymro Cymraeg): The same as a WELSH WELSHMAN, as opposed to a WELSHMAN who is unable to speak Welsh or WELSHLESS.

**'Welsh-speaking Welshwoman'** ('Cymraes' or 'Cymraes Gymraeg'): Eg. N. Jones uses this term (1993:130,172).

**Welsh speech:** Like WELSH TONGUE, a synonym for the WELSH LANGUAGE.

**Welsh Speedwell** (veronica hybrida): Or bugle-leafed speedwell. Also called WELSH SPIKED SPEEDWELL. A plant endemic to Wales.

**Welsh Spellchecker:** CYSILL 2 – produced by the WELSH LANGUAGE BOARD and used for word processor (Yr Enfys, Winter 1995/6 p.17).

**Welsh spiked speedwell:** See WELSH SPEEDWELL.

**Welsh spindle sheaths:**

**Welsh Spinning Wheel** (Y Droell Fawr – 'The Great Wheel'). The old C14th spinning wheel is often referred to as the 'Welsh Spinning Wheel' (eg. J.G. Jenkins 1981:25). This unique Welsh device replaced the spindle and in turn was superseded by the smaller flyer wheel and eventually spinning jennies. It was turned with the right hand while the left hand held carded fibres.

**'Welsh Spirit of the Mines', The:** As the WELSH MINE GOBLINS (qv.) are also called (A. Jones 1995:118).

**Welsh spooner:** See WELSH SPOON CARVER.

**Welsh Spoon Carver** (naddwr [llwyau]): The maker of the WELSH LOVESPOON (qv.) (J. Geraint Jenkins Folk Life 1:39). The term is more exact than WELSH SPOONER since this could also be applied to one who gives (rather than makes) a WELSH LOVE SPOON ('spooning' meaning courting). One of the unique cutting tools which the Welsh Spoon carver uses is the 'twca cam'.

**Welsh sporting thriller:** Bell's term for a genre of Welsh fiction (NWR 4:75, 1989).

**Welsh Sports Hall of Fame:** Roll of Honour for great Welsh sportsmen at the Museum of WELSH LIFE, St Fagans.

**Welsh springer:** See WELSH SPRINGER SPANIEL.

**Welsh spring lamb:** A young WELSH LAMB (born in Spring).

**Welsh Springer Spaniel** (Torfgi Cymreig): A unique breed of Welsh Spaniel. cf. WELSH CORGI, WELSH FOXHOUND, WELSH TERRIER.

**Welsh springer spaniel Staffordshire dogs:** Among the famous collectors' Staffordshire figures (listed by Pope 1990:160-1).

**Welsh Squaddies:** Neil Evans with reference to Karl Francis' *Milwr Bychan* talks of 'The triangle of the political establishment, Welsh Squaddies and Irish insurgents' (Planet 80:93).

**Welsh squirearchy:** eg. In R. Rees Davies' *Owain Glyndŵr and the Welsh Squirearchy*.

**Welsh's spitzenberg:** One of the many synonyms of Red Canada, a variety of Canadian apple.

**Welsh stallion:** See WELSH SIRE.

**Welsh stamps:** Welsh stamps differ from English stamps in that they have a small dragon in the top left hand corner (Ulster stamps have a hand and Scottish stamps a lion – Manx, Irish, Jersey & Guernsey stamps, however, are completely different). In addition to the common Welsh stamps, there have been special stamps issued: eg. the stamp featuring the 'WELSH WATER SPANIEL/Torfgi Cymreig' 10½, 1979). One Christmas series featured 'The Tanad Valley Plygain 18p'. In 1988 there was a whole series of 4 stamps featuring the WELSH BIBLE with Bishop Morgan et al. in English and Welsh. The 'Dolwyddelan, Gwynedd, Cymru/Wales' 41p stamp was another, as was the 'Pontcysyllte Aqueduct, Clwyd' 35p. In 1994 a series featured one Welsh stamp '19p Amser Haf

Summertime, Llanelwedd'. The 'Castell y Waun, Chirk Castle, Clwyd, Cymru was another and the 'Caernarfon Castle £1.50' stamp has long been popular for sending small parcels. cf. WELSH BULL, BLACK; WELSH POUND.

**Welsh Standing Committee:** See WELSH WHITE PAPER.

**'Welsh star slime'** (pwdre sêr, ie. 'star powder'): A substance found on the ground and was once associated with shooting stars but is in fact the gelatinous remains of frog's/toad's oviducts. In Dyfed it is called 'godro'r sêr' (milkings of the stars) (Morris 1910:145). cf. WELSH SNAKE STONE.

**Welsh Stew:** Made with added home-cured bacon as well as beef, potatoes, onions, carrots and swede (John Jones 1994:15).

**Welsh Stick:** One name for the WELSH NOT (qv.).

**'Welsh stick chair':** Type of chair made in Wales, with sticks instead of a piece of wood for the back and usually with three legs. Especially popular in C18th and early C19th and made of ash and elm (see J. Brown 1990).

**Welsh Stokholm:** The island off S.W. Dyfed with Britain's first bird observatory, as opposed to the capital of Sweden (Stockholm).

**'Welsh stone':** As coal is called. cf. 'Scotch stone' which is Ayr stone. See WELSH COAL, WELSH DIAMOND, WELSH PEARL.

**Welsh Street:** One of the streets leading to the Town Gate in Casgwent (Chepstow) and 'a reminder that the Welsh were not allowed to live within the town' (in tourist pamphlet *The Walled Towns of Wales and Chester*. cf. WELSH ROAD, WELSH WAY etc.

**'Welsh strict metres':** The term refers to poetry which is written in unique Welsh metrical forms eg. 'cynghanedd', 'cywydd' and 'englyn' etc.

**'Welsh Strike', The:** This historical term refers to two episodes: 1) In Scranton, the WELSH ATHENS 'When miners went on strike in December, 1870. The often violent, six-month walk-out took on ethnic overtones and became known as the "Welsh Strike" ' (Petro: 1994:108). 2) The 'Cambrian Strike' (1910-11) referring to the Tonypandy Riots.

**Welsh stud:** WELSH PONY STALLION. The WELSH STUD book gives information about only the four pure breeds: WELSH MOUNTAIN PONY, WELSH PONY, WELSH PONY OF COB TYPE and WELSH COB. It does not include information about WELSH PART BRED stallions.

**Welsh Stud Book,' 'a Walking:** So Alison Mountain, Chairman of the WELSH PONY AND COB SOCIETY calls Wynne Davies in the forward of his book (1993:6).

**Welsh Studies:** A separate subject discipline comprising WELSH LANGUAGE and WELSH ETHNOLOGY etc. There is a professor of Welsh Studies and terms like Welsh Studies Conference (of NWAF), and the University of Rio Grande, OH. Welsh Studies Conference. There is also the term Welsh Studies Unit.

**Welsh-style:** (Adj.) in a Welsh style.

**Welsh-styled:** (Adj.) Styled in a Welsh fashion. cf. WELSH-STYLE.

**Welsh Subalps:** Those Welsh mountains not quite as high as the WELSH ALPS and outside the main range of Snowdonia. John of Salisbury wrote in 1157 'The English king has set out to conquer the Welsh amidst their Alps and sub-Alps' (quoted by Stephens ed. 1992:6).

**Welsh subdialect:** The regional variation of a WELSH DIALECT (qv.) eg. the difference of one part of Dyfed to another.

**Welsh sub-kings:** The lesser Welsh kings as opposed to the WELSH HIGH KING. O.J. Padel uses this term (1978:23).

**Welsh Sugar Loaf:** As the Sugar Loaf Mountain near Abergavenny can be called to distinguish it from the one in Rio de Janeiro or the Irish Sugar Loaf in Co. Wicklow.

**Welsh Suibhne Geilt:** Ellis makes this parallel between the

Irish king cursed by St Ronán and transformed into a bird in the forest leaping from tree to tree and Myrddin Wyllt (1992:165,200). Indeed, perhaps there is an etymological connection with Geilt (Ir. 'grazing') and Wyllt (> W. gwyllt – 'wild' and by extension 'mad').

**Welsh subtitles** (is-deitlau): For English programmes can be seen from p.889 of Sbectel. Some Welsh films eg. Hedd Wyn have subtitles in English.

**Welsh Summer houses** (tai haf, sing. tŷ haf): As distinct from the 'hafotai' or agricultural summer dwellings used for transhumant animal farmers, the 'tai haf' are 'summer houses' usually belonging to English occupants in Wales and are unoccupied in the winter. They are resented by many Welsh people, especially those houses in the WELSH HEARTLAND. Over 200 such houses have been burnt by extremists, mainly Meibion Glyndŵr.

**Welsh Summer School** (Ysgol Haf): As Nant Gwrtheyrn (and other such schools) are called where WELSH LEARNERS gather for intensive courses in Welsh in the summer and residing on campus.

**'Welsh Sunday':** Talking of the Sabbath institution, Rees writes 'The Puritan Sunday, or the "Welsh Sunday" as it is now often called, remains both as an ideal and in practice' (1996:128).

**Welsh Sunday Closing Act** (1881): Or Welsh Closing Act. This forbade innkeepers to sell alcohol on Sunday, except to bona fide travellers. The 'Dry Sunday' had come in response to the demand from many chapels to 'boddi'r cynhaeaf' (drown the harvest) ie. get rid of all drinking festivals etc. Yet ironically, before many chapels were built, meetings were often held in public houses. The government decided to extend it to Monmouthshire in 1921.

**Welsh Supreme in-Hand Champion, Old Mill:** Title for WELSH PONY champion in The Royal Agricultural Winter Fair, Toronto, Canada (see WPCSJ 1991:172).

**'Welsh Sweater'** (Y Sweter Cymreig): A unique type of sweater, resembling the Fisherman's Sweater (Sutton 1987:87). It has a pattern all over the top with 'seams of coal, hearts (from the WELSH LOVE-SPOONS) and the cabled ropes of fishermen'. Not to be confused with WELSH JUMPERS (a nickname for the WELSH METHODISTS).

**Welsh swine:** Phrase used by Sikes for WELSH PIG (1880:108). See also WELSH WHITE.

**Welsh Table Wine:** Produced at Parva Farm Vineyards near Tintern Abbey. cf. WELSH WHISKY, WELSH 'VIGNERONS', WELSH WINE.

**'Welsh taboo story':** A category of Welsh fairy tale (Elias Owen 1887:16,24) in which a taboo is imposed. cf. The 'geis' in Irish myths.

**'Welsh Taffy':** A tautology. Geraint H. Jenkins quoting the English stereotypes writes 'The poor "Welsh Taffy" was a liar and a thief' (1996:8).

**Welsh Talgarth:** (Encycl. Brit.) In Brecon, there was both an English Talgarth and Welsh Talgarth (in the latter WELSH LAWS prevailed).

**Welsh-talking:** (Adj.) (of a person, film, programme) which talks Welsh.

**Welsh tall hat** (yr het dal): See WELSH HAT.

**Welsh tampoy:** James Williams referring to gorse flower wine writes 'This was the Welsh tampoy, gorse flowers being picked instead of gilliflowers' (1973:14).

**Welsh tapestry:** Not a tapestry but refers to bed covers and quilts. Sutton writes 'The word "tapestry" is used in Wales, erroneously, to describe a double-cloth fabric where two cloths are woven simultaneously, one on top of the other . . . '. The most famous type of bed cover in Wales is the 'carthen'. cf. WELSH CARPET. By extension, there are unique Welsh crafts such as 'Welsh tapestry bedspreads', 'Welsh tapestry purses' and 'Welsh tapestry stools' etc. ('Wales: Crafts and Rural

Industries', Wales Tourist Board, 1976:10,20,23).

**'Welsh tartan'** (brithwe): The type of plaid used in WELSH COSTUME. cf. WELSH KILT.

**'Welshtbreton':** Word used by James Joyce in *Finnegans Wake* (Ch.XV). It is an Anglo-Irish contraction of 'West Briton' (Wall 1987:106). It is a paradox that the association of this word with Welsh is not in the prefix 'Welsht-' but in the '-breton' part (> Ir. Breatnach-Welsh, Bhreatain Bheag, an -Wales ie. 'Small Britain').

**Welsh tea:** In tea shops in Wales 'Welsh tea' is a pot of tea served with WELSH CAKES, butter and jam.

**'Welsh Tea Bread':** As Freeman calls 'bara brith' (speckled fruit bread) which is indispensable to a traditional WELSH TEA (1996:102).

**Welsh tea towel:** One of the popular souvenir items.

**Welsh-Tehuelche:** (Adj.) That which pertains to both the WELSH SETTLERS and The Tehuelche (native Indians of Patagonia). The Welsh always cultivated friendly relations with the Indians and at times intervened on their behalf with the Argentine government.

**Welsh terrier:** Type of terrier in Wales. The Scots also have their own 'Scotch terrier' and the Irish their 'Irish terrier'. The Sealyham is a type of terrier from Pembrokeshire, most similar to the Lakeland terrier. cf. WELSH CORGI, WELSH FOXHOUND, WELSH SPRINGER SPANIEL.

**'Welsh Terror', The Little:** Jimmy Wilde (1892-1969). World flyweight champion. Also called the 'Tylorstown Terror' (as he came from Tylorstown, Rhondda) and the 'Mighty Atom'. Other great Welsh World champions include Howard Winston who won the world featherweight title in 1968 (see the WELSH WIZARD). Freddie Welsh (Frederick Hall Thomas 1886-1927), World lightweight champion (1914). Colin Jones drew the World Welterweight title in 1983.

**'Welsh Thing', The** (Y Pethe Cymraeg): K. Gramich writes

'David Jones evidently irritated some English critics with his uncompromising insistence on what he called "The Welsh Thing" . . . ' (with reference to Welsh allusions, unintelligible to an English audience) (Planet 114:80, Dec.1995/Jan.1996).

**Welsh-thinking:** (Adj.) Thinking like a WELSHMAN.

**'Welsh Thinking Cap':** See WELSH WISHING CAP.

**Welsh 3,000s:** The fourteen peaks in N. Wales which are over 3,000 ft (Unsworth 1975:360). In Scotland a peak over 3,000 is called a 'munro', whereas one between 2,500-3,000 is a 'Corbett'. The 'Scottish 4,000s' are four peaks in the Cairngorms and three in the Ben Nevis group. See WELSH ALPS, WELSH HIGHLANDS, WELSH HOLY MOUNTAIN, WELSH MATTERHORN, WELSH RABBITS, SOCIETY OF, WELSH SUBALPS, WELSH TIGER.

**'Welsh Tiger':** Also 'The First Tiger' – Owen Glynne Jones (1867-99). Science teacher and pioneer of British mountain climbing. He was killed when his guide Furrer fell attempting the Ferpécle arête (henceforth known as the Jones arête). cf. WELSH RABBITS, SOCIETY OF.

**Welsh-tinted:** Joseph P. Clancy uses the expression 'through Welsh-tinted glasses' (NWR 32:37, Spring 1996), ie. looking at things through a welsh persepctive.

**Welsh Tit Bits:** A column in the Cardiff Times (Davies 1911:247,284), not a Welsh version of the magazine 'Tit Bits'.

**Welsh toast:** Yackeeda! (really 'iechyd da' – 'good health').

**'Welsh toasted cheese'** (Tost Caws): Not WELSH RABBIT (qv.) but a recipe of toasted WELSH CAERPHILLY with toast and served with raw onion (WELSH ONION?) (see Smeeth 1994:109).

**'Welsh toffee':** Welsh version of toffee prepared from butter, sugar, vinegar and golden syrup. As it was being cooled, put on hearthstone (Grant 1993:60). See WELSH TOFFEE EVENING.

**'Welsh toffee evening'** (Noson Gyflaith): An evening around Christmas time when family and friends gathered around fire telling stories etc. while toffee was being made. Smith-Twiddy writes that 'cyflaith' 'was often made for the "calennig children" who called to wish the family a happy New Year' (1979:78).

**Welsh Tom Tit Stories:** A category of Welsh legends so called by Rhys (1901:583-4).

**Welshton:** Or Welchton, La – a place name.

**'Welsh tongue':** WELSH LANGUAGE.

**Welsh top hat:** See WELSH HAT.

**'Welsh Tour', The:** Or less commonly, The 'Tour of Wales'. The late C18th and mainly C19th phenomenon of English visitors going on a tour of Wales. A.J. Lewis writes 'The Welsh tour and its accompaniment, the travelogue, first became popular in the mid-eighteenth century' (1994-95:29). Indeed many subesquently wrote about their experiences. See WELSH CRUISE, WELSH HERITAGE TOUR, WELSH TOURISTS.

**Welsh Tourist Board** (Bwrdd Croeso Cymru lit. 'Welcome Board of Wales'): It should be Wales Tourist Board.

**'Welsh tourists':** Really English tourists who went on the WELSH TOUR. Many writers eg. Bingley in 1800 (quoted by Kirk 1994:106) used the term.

**Welsh Tourists, Father of:** Or 'Father of The Cambrian Tourists' (Yr Enfys, Spring 1997 p.4) Epithet for Thomas Pennant (1726-98).

**'Welsh Town':** The meaning of Walton (Piehler 1935:121).

**Welsh Tract, The** (Y Rhandir Gymraeg): A piece of land in N.W. Philadelphia, promised to WELSH QUAKER immigrants by William Penn to have an independent government by Welsh Magistrates in Welsh. It was to include townships of Upper and Lower Meirion, Haverford, Radnor, Tredyffrin, E. and W. Whiteland, E. & W. Goshen, Williston, E. Town and part of W. Town. The promise was betrayed and other settlers came. See WELSH-AMERICAN, WELSH ATHENS OF AMERICA,

WELSH 'BARONY'.

**Welsh-trained:** Trained in Wales or by Welsh people. May writes that Grand National winning horse Royal Mail (ridden by Evans Williams in 1937) was 'Welsh-owned and Welsh-trained' (1994:223). cf. WELSH COB, WELSH PONY etc.

**'Welsh Trainspotting':** Peter Morgan writes of Kevin Allen's film – '*Twin Town* has been dubbed "The Welsh Trainspotting" ' (NWR 37:82, 1997).

**Welsh Tramping Road:** Gwyn Jones writes 'The Long Welsh Tramping Road leads up from Fernal to the mansions of High Eden' (1955:254; also 246,260). cf. WELSH DROVERS' WAY, WELSH NASH WAY, WELSH ROAD, WELSH WAY.

**'Welsh Travellers':** A misnomer for Irish Travellers living in Wales. qv. WELSH QUARTER. cf. WELSH GYPSIES.

**Welsh Triads, The** (Trioedd Ynys Prydein): No relation to the WELSH MAFFIA (Taffia). A literary work (see Bromwich trans. 1961) with characters, horses etc. from Welsh legends catalogued in threes. The number three was very important to the Welsh. Interestingly ap Dafydd tells us that in Nefyn, herrings were counted in a unit of three called a 'mwrw' (1988:35-6) or 'bwrw; (G.P.C., p.356).

**'Welsh Trilateral', The:** Three castles: White, Skenfrith and Grosmont, all granted by King John to Hubert de Burgh in 1201 (see A. & C. Black 'Wales: Blue Guide', 7th edit. 1990:193-7).

**Welsh trilogy:** A series of three Welsh novels, especially those of Alexander Cordell (1914-97) who has completed two such trilogies (see Planet 125:128, 1997).

**Welsh triple:** For many WELSH HARPISTS eg. Ellis (1991:50) 'Welsh triples' refers to WELSH TRIPLE HARPS.

**Welsh triple harp** (telyn deires): The most common form of WELSH HARP (qv. see Buines 1992:149 who prefer this term).

**Welsh Triple Harpist** (Telynor Teires Cymreig): Harpist who plays the WELSH TRIPLE HARP (The term is used in Yr Enfys, Winter 1996/97, p.7).

**Welsh Tripple Harp:** Alternative spelling of WELSH TRIPLE HARP (qv.), (used in Yr Enfys, Winter 1996/97, p.9).

**Welsh triple stringed harp:** As the WELSH TRIPLE HARP is sometimes called (eg. M. Roberts 1992:23).

**Welsh troubadors:** (Stephens ed. 1986:518). The cler?

**'Welsh Trout in Bacon':** A unique Welsh recipe of trout filled with butter, parsley, lemon slice and pepper wrapped with rashers of bacon then grilled and chopped chives added. Served with vegetables and 'minted peas' (see Howells, p.45).

**'Welsh trumpet':** Trumpet (horn) used at the Cornish Gorseth and was a present from Wales. The Corn Gwlad.

**Welsh Trust:** A fund est. by Thomas Gouge in 1674 to provide elementary schools to teach Welsh children to read and write (in English). However, the Welsh Trust also supplied Welsh religious books and in 1677 published a new WELSH BIBLE.

**'Welsh turncoat':** Geraint H. Jenkins refers to 'The Stock Welsh Turncoat known as Dic Sion Dafydd, the pseudo-gentleman who affected an English accent whenever he espied the River Severn . . . ' (1996:9).

**Welsh TV Times:** Sbec, the Welsh-language magazine giving details of Welsh T.V. programmes, yet unlike T.V. Times incorporates information of some BBC programmes as well as WELSH FOURTH CHANNEL. N. Jones calls it 'The Welsh equivalent of TV Times' (1993:167).

**Welsh tweed** (brethyn Cymru): Welsh woollen material similar to Scots tweed (> tweed, twill, but perh. influenced by the River Tweed).

**Welsh-type:** (Adj.) Of a type like the Welsh, WELSH-LIKE.

**'Welsh Type', The:** 'Y bobl fach ddu', the 'genuine' characteristic Welsh person short and dark as the original WELSH CELTS. (Beatrix Potter p.122-Voriks.)

**Welsh Ulysses:** Brân or Bendigeidfran. In The Mabinogion he went to Ireland, his body forming a bridge across the sea over which his Welsh followers crossed to Ireland to avenge his sister Branwen. In Irish legend Bran sails to The Isles of the Otherworld in 'The Voyage of Brân'.

**'Welsh uncle':** (Brewer – under the entry 'uncle'). 'The husband of a parent's cousin: sometimes a first cousin'. There is no equivalent of a 'parent's cousin' in English; yet kinship terms exist in some other cultures eg. 'fille onkel' in Norwegian (fem. fille tante) and 'osaba txiki' (literally 'little uncle') in Basque. Some primitive cultures eg. Hawaiian also have equivalents.

**Welsh underpitch vault:** See WELSH VAULT.

**Welsh Undersecretary:** Or Welsh Office Undersecretary. See WELSH SECRETARY.

**'Welsh Underworld':** Annwn. See WELSH OTHERWORLD.

**Welsh Unionist Party:** A political party (Dwelly's Appendix p.36).

**Welsh Unionists:** Term used for those WELSHPEOPLE (as opposed to WELSH NATIONALISTS) who prefer to be part of the U.K. (eg. used by Royston Jones in *The Link*, No.2, Y Monitor Cymreig Vol.1, No.4, July/Aug. 1996). cf. Ulster Unionists.

**'Welsh Unit':** As local WELSH NURSERY groups are usually called.

**Welsh United** (Cymru Unedig):

**'Welsh Uplands':** A term used (eg. by Peate 1972:58 and J. Geraint Jenkins 1990:36) for the WELSH HIGHLANDS.

**Welsh Valentine:** See WELSH ST VALENTINE.

**'Welsh Valleys':** The phrase is applied to the valleys of South Wales, associated with mining and once an important part of the WELSH HEARTLAND. There are still WELSH-SPEAKING areas in the Welsh Valleys. One also speaks of a 'Valleys accent' (ie. particular type of Welsh accent typical of this area).

**Welsh vaticinatory verse** (canu brud): Under English

subjucation, a form of prophetic Welsh poetry centred on a 'mab darogan' or 'daroganwr' who will come and redeem his people (see R.W. Evans 1979).

**Welsh vault:** An underpitch vault. cf. WELSH ARCH, WELSH GROIN.

**Welsh-vaulted:** With a WELSH VAULT.

**Welsh vaulting:** The making of a WELSH VAULT (qv.).

**'Welsh Veal Sauce'** (Suryn Cyffaith Poeth): A unique Welsh recipe with lemon, horseradish, salt, garlic, mace, nutmeg, cayenne, mustard and vinegar (Grant 1993:61).

**'Welsh Vegetable par excellence', The:** As Collins and Pawnall call the WELSH LEEK (1988:132).

**Welsh-veneered:** John Osmond's phrase to refer to something with a Welsh veneer (Planet 48:5, May 1979).

**'Welsh Veto', The:** As the Welsh reaction to the WELSH REFERENDUM (qv.) is called.

**Welsh vice-counties:** As the 'old' thirteen counties of Wales are sometimes called (eg. National Museum of Wales Catalogue 1993, p.45).

**Welsh 'Vignerons':** Welsh vine growers. Wynford Vaughan-Thomas says of Castell Coch vineyard 'You can imagine the grapes ripening happily and the Welsh 'vignerons' singing . . . ' (1981:151).

**Welsh Viking:** Raymond Garlick uses the epithet as a title for his review of Gwyn Jones' *Background to Dylan Thomas and Other Explorations* (Planet 95:93-4, Oct./Nov. 1992). Garlick ends review with quote 'I am also a Welsh Viking'.

**Welshville:** Place name.

**'Welsh violin':** Roderick (1986:103) refers to the 'crwth' as 'a king of Welsh violin'. Not to be confused with the WELSH FIDDLE (qv.).

**Welsh Virgil, The:** Matthews & Matthews write 'Often translated as the Fairies, Fferyllt is probably derived from the

Welsh for Virgil, 'Fferyll', who had a reputation in medieval times for being a magician and alchemist' (and is modern Welsh for 'chemist') (1988:74).

**Welsh Virgins, 11,000:** The 11,000 Virgins of Cologne who were killed.

**'Welsh Volcano':** As Holland (1992:53) designates Moelfamma(u), a high mountain near Holywell, Flintshire which, according to letters in 'Bye-gones' (1773, 1877 and 1885) made a rumbling noise like an eruption, and in July 1877 lava actually spilt from it killing two people.

**'Welsh vole':** A unique subspecies of vole found only on the island of Skomer off Pembrokeshire.

**Welsh Voltaire:** As Geraint H. Jenkins calls scholar and political thinker William Jones, Llangudfad (1726-95) (The Celtic Pen, Vol.3, Issue 1, p.11, Winter 1995-96).

**Welsh 'W':** In Welsh 'w' is a vowel when placed between consonant and sound like 'oo' in book. If circumflexed eg. cŵn (dogs) it is longer like 'oo' in cool. In some dialects, eg. Dyfed 'wh' is a separate letter (Morris 1910).

**'Welsh Wainwright', The:** On the back cover of Chris Barber's book *The Seven Hills of Abergavenny* (Blorenge Books, 1992), the reviewer writes of the author 'He is sometimes referred to as the "Welsh Wainwright".'

**'Welsh Wake':** Term used by C. Stevens (1976:30) which is analogous with the Irish wake and refers to the 'gwylnos' or 'watch night' which was the vigil kept by the gwylwyr (mourners, lit. 'watchers') around the dead on the eve of the funeral. At the tŷ corff or house of the dead, many games and amusements were played and food and ale consumed, making the merrymaking Irish connotations of the word 'wake' an apt parallel of the Welsh equivalent.

**'Welsh Wake nights':** J.C. Davies uses this term (1911:41) in much the same way that Stevens uses WELSH WAKE (qv.).

**Welsh Wales** (Y Fro Gymraeg): See WELSH HEARTLAND.

**Welsh War of Independence, The Third:** As May calls Owain Glyndŵr's Rebellion of 1400 (1994:324). See WELSH WARS OF INDEPENDENCE (First and Second).

**Welsh War Poets:** Welsh counterparts of the English War Poets of W.W.1., notably Hedd Wyn.

**Welsh War, The First:** See WELSH WARS.

**Welsh War, The Second:** See WELSH WARS.

**Welshware:** See WELSH WARE.

**'Welsh ware':** Term used by Miller and Miller for 'Late C18 and C19, rustic flatware, decorated with trailed and combed slip' (1990:154). cf. WELSH LACQUER.

**Welsh Warehouse, Royal:** Built in Newtown, 1861. First mail-order business in the world – est. by Pryce Jones for WELSH FLANNEL.

**'Welsh Warrior-Statesman', The:** So Owain Glyndŵr is called (in Mid Wales Festival of the Countryside: Official Guide 1991:42). See WELSH REBEL HERO.

**Welsh Wars:** Or the Welsh Wars of Independence. The 1st Welsh War was 1276-7 and the 2nd Welsh War 1282-3, fought between Llywelyn (ap Gruffudd ein Llyw Olaf) and the English under Edward I. The Welsh after heroic attempts were defeated in both wars and henceforth Welsh subjugation to England was intersified by the Statute of Rhuddlan which followed in 1284.

**'Welsh Washer of The Ford':** The Gwrach y Rhibyn (Leach 1949:142,203). See WELSH BANSHEE.

**'Welsh Wasps':** So Newport Rugby Team have been called because of their black and amber striped shirts.

**Welsh wassail pot/bowl:** Large bowl made by Ewenny for containing ale at the Christmas season.

**Welsh-Watching:** By analogy with Desmond Morris' 'Man-watching', Welsh-watching is a term which can refer to anthropological case studies of the Welsh. It is coined by Nerys Thomas Patterson and used as the title of her review of

American anthropologist Carol Trosset's book *Welshness Performed: Welsh Concepts of Person and Society* (Planet 107:97-8, Oct./Nov. 1994).

**'Welsh water fays':** Loomis' term for the fairies associated with lakes eg. The Lady of Little Van Lake (Leach ed. 1949:748).

**'Welsh Water-horse':** As the 'ceffyl y dŵr' is often called (eg. Elias Owen 1887:138). This is a beautiful horse which takes its rider to his death by plunging into the sea. Only a clergyman can ride it. It corresponds with the Manx 'cabbyl-ushtey' and 'Glashtin', Scottish 'kelpie' (hence Rhys refers to a 'Cambrian Kelpie', 1901:242-3), / Gaelic 'each uisage', Ir. eac uisge and Shetland 'shoopiltee' or 'njuggle', Orkney 'tang(ie)' and in the Faroes 'nykur' etc.

**Welsh water monster:** The 'afanc' or 'addanc' which means 'beaver'. It dwelt off the River Conway in the Llyn yr Afanc and dragged people and animals into lake to die. In one story it was slain by Peredur who used a magic stone to make him invisible. cf. WELSH WATER HORSE.

**Welsh wave** (venusia cambricaria): Also called Weaver's Wave – a moth (which like another endemic species 'Ashworth's rustic') is only to be found in certain hilly regions of N. Wales. cf. WELSH CLEARWING.

**Welsh way, The:** One of the main WELSH DROVERS' routes. Elias writes 'Gellid un ai dilyn hen lwybrau drwy'r Cotswolds am Buckingham neu gyfeirio at Gaerloyw a dilyn yr hen "Ermine Street" Rufeinig a'r ffordd a elwid y "Welsh Way" heibio Cirencester ac yna ar hyd y Berkshire Ridgeway a oedd yn rhydd o dollbyrth' (1987:37). cf. 'The Cambrian Way' – Cardiff to Conway (Parker and Whitfield 1997:400).

**'Welsh web':** 1) With reference to kinds of knitted wear, M.E. Jones writes 'Welsh "webs" and "flannels" were marketed by English middlemen' (1978:40). 2) Kevin Williams calls Internet 'The Welsh Web' (Planet 115:28, Feb./March 1996).

**'Welsh Wedding Procession':** At the International Welsh Show

Denmark (18th-19th Aug. 1990) one of the features was 'The Welsh Wedding Procession, made of WELSH PONIES and COBS of all sections and all actors dressed up in WELSH NATIONAL COSTUMES . . . ' (WPCSJ 1991:180).

**Welsh Week:** 1) A week eg. Miri Awst organised by CYD at Nantgwrtheyrn devoted to the WELSH LANGUAGE. 2) A week of Welsh cultural events eg. The New Quay 'Welsh Week' 2-9 July, 1991.

**Welsh Weekend:** A weekend organised for learners to get together and improve their Welsh.

**Welsh Weinling:** More commonly spelt Welsch Weinling or known as Welschisner, an apple variety. cf. WELSH BEAUTY, WELSH PIPPIN etc.

**'Welsh welcome mat':** As David Jones refers to Max Munday's willingness to cooperate with Japanese manufacturers and investers' (Planet 83:94, Oct./Nov. 1990).

**'Welsh Welsh':** See WELSH GLOBAL.

**Welsh Welshman** (Cymro Cymraeg): The same as WELSH-SPEAKING WELSHMAN (qv.).

**'Welsh Wench of the Day:** By allusion to the Sun's 'Page 3', Dylan Iorwerth refers to 'The nipples of the Welsh Wench of the Day on page 3 of Rupert Murdoch's "Yr Haul" ' (Planet 118:96, Aug./Sept.1996). See WELSH WILD CAT.

**Welsh weregild':** So 'galanas' has been called. This was payment to relatives in compensation for murder or manslaughter according to the old WELSH LAWS and was abolished by Dafydd. It corresponds with the Irish 'eric' ('éraic'), Scots 'kelchyn' and Norse 'mannebot', etc. Similarly 'sarhäed' was compensation for injury and 'wynebwerth' was a compensation for an insult.

**'Welsh West',** The: G. Evans writes of the Welsh 'They all lived in the part of Britain that Gildas called Britannia, an early example of the limitation of this term to the Welsh West'

(1974:71). Not to be confused with the 'West Welsh' (ie. Cornish).

**Welsh Westminster Abbey:** As Barber tells us (1992:55), 'A Victorian writer once descibed St Mary's (Abergavenny) as the 'Westminster Abbey of South Wales' so impressed was he with its fine monuments, tombs and mural tablets'.

**Welsh Wheat Stook:** (W. Bwch) An ornamental stook of wheat (somewhat distinct from the WELSH FAN qv.) and tied with bands and ribbons. Lady Llanover drew one in her *Good Cookery* (1867, 256, plate 5). cf. WELSH BARLEY SHEAF.

**'Welsh Whim', The** (Y Chwiw Cymraeg): A Welsh dance tune.

**'Welsh Whisky':** Spelt like the Scotch 'whisky' rather than the Irish 'whiskey' (and 'Manx Whiskey'). A Scot Mr Colville started a Welsh whisky industry. The labels on the bottles had a painting of Jenny Jones in WELSH COSTUME and verse:

'Why with capers so many
John Jones, gay you are
Welsh Whisky, dear Jenny
From Bala, bur dda.'

From 1980s 'Sŵn y Môr' (Sound of the Sea) Welsh Whisky' was produced. Jack Daniel is also reputed to be Welsh. cf. WELSH WINE.

**'Welsh Whisky King:** Dafydd Gittins who founded WELSH WHISKY business in 1976 and who also started WELSH MEAD.

**Welsh white:** See WELSH WHITE BREED.

**Welsh white breed:** 1) Or simply 'WELSH' or 'WELSH PIG', a lop-eared breed of pig like Landrace. 2) Also type of cattle with white colouring as opposed to WELSH BLACKS (qv.).

**Welsh white flannel:** As Kendall refers to the type of WELSH FLANNEL from Abergavenny (I.G.W. 1989:103).

**Welsh Whitehall:** 1) Roy Clews (1980:158) calls the WELSH OFFICE (qv.) 'The mini-Whitehall of Wales'. Or, as Deacon calls it, 'The Pox Box for Whitehall' (Planet 117:42, 1996). 2) Maud writes of O.M. Edwards' house Neuadd Wen in Llanuwchllyn, 'That it was his own "Whitehall" in Wales' (1994:93).

**'Welsh White Indians':** As the WELSH INDIANS are sometimes called (14.452d).

**Welsh white lie stories** (storïau celwydd golau): A genre of witty storytelling as done by Shemi Wad and other experts, involving fantastic exaggeration as well as humour, the storïwr often telling incredible stories of his own exploits, flying through air etc.

**Welsh White Paper:** As Rosser writes 'Ness Edwards had recommended that the government's annual Welsh White Paper and the Welsh Digest of Statistics should be discussed in a Welsh Standing Committee which would meet for six mornings in each parliamentary session' (1987:70).

**'Welsh whore':** A Bristol man was supposed to be 'The son of an Irish thief and a Welch whore' (DHS). cf. WELSH BEDDING, WELSH WIFE.

**Welsh-wide:** Or Wales-wide, throughout Wales.

**'Welsh wife':** A loose woman. cf. Dutch widow (harlot). Originally a 'Welsh wife' was a 'common law wife' – perhaps from the old custom of 'byw tali' (cohabit without marriage) (cf. The Irish 'talley woman' – Irish mistress/girl of an English Lord, Hickey & Doherty 1980:558). In O. Welsh a 'gordderch' meant concubine, adultress or sweetheart. cf. WELSH BEDDING, WELSH WHORE.

**Welsh wig:** A knitted skull cap (eg. Harris 1980:133; and Etheridge 1990:97-9).

**Welsh Wild Cat:** A Welsh model Siân who has posed topless for the Sun Page 3 (and other things, apparently?). cf. WELSH WENCH OF THE DAY.

**'Welsh Will o' The Wisp':** As Briggs calls the 'Ellylldan' (1976:121), type of Welsh sprite like the spunkie or Jack Lantern, often misleading travellers. See WELSH CORPSE CANDLE.

**'Welsh willow pattern':** The lustrous blue designs on meat dishes and plates etc., mostly associated with Swansea pottery.

**Welsh Wimpy:** As there are so-called Hawaiian Wimpies (with pineapple slice) and Mexican ones (with chilli sauce) etc., why not, as Palfrey and Roberts suggest, 'try the Welsh Wimpy – compressed chitterlings and laverbread served up in a bap' (1994:18).

**'Welsh Windbag':** As Tariq Ali called Labour leader Neil Kinnock in 1984, an epithet also applied to David Lloyd George (quoted by Stephens ed. 1992:162). cf. WELSH WIZARD.

**'Welsh wine':** Or 'The Wine of Wales' – metheglin (meddyglyn), a Welsh fermented honey drink like mead. cf. WELSH HOGSWASH, WELSH TABLE WINE, WELSH WHISKY.

**'Welsh winged serpent':** The 'gwiber', a flying snake which drinks women's milk. cf. WELSH DRAGON.

**Welsh-wise:** As regard Welsh.

**'Welsh wishing caps':** Roderick writes 'Welsh wishing caps or hats were made from hazel leaves and twigs though sometimes juniper sprigs and berries would be used. With caps on the head it was possible therefore to make any wish come true but, to be really effective, the twigs and leaves had to be picked at midnight under the new moon . . . If the wearer so wished the wishing or thinking cap would make him or her invisible' (1986:72-3). cf. Ger. Tarn Kappe and Norw. usynlighetshatt.

**'Welsh witch's hat':** Villiers' phrase (1965:755) for the WELSH HAT (qv.).

**Welsh Wizard, The:** This epithet has been applied to many WELSHMEN: 1) David Lloyd George (1863-1945) prime-minister. cf. WELSH CAESAR AUGUSTUS, WELSHMAN, THE LITTLE, WELSH WINDBAG. The best etymology I've read: Palfrey and Roberts suggest David Lloyd George's epithet was coined 'Probably because he miraculously changed himself from a fervent Welsh Nationalist into a royalist sycophant within a matter of a few years' (1994:56). 2) Dylan Thomas (1914-53), poet and prose-writer. Wynford Vaughan Thomas refers to him as 'The Wild Welsh Wizard' (1981:104); and in 1962 Gwyn Thomas had also written of this great writer 'in his short days on earth was as much a wizard as Merlin' (quoted by Stephens ed. 1992:132). 3) Howard Winstone, world featherweight champion in 1968. His sobriquet 'The Welsh Wizard' is the title of his biography by Les Miles (Concept Associates Ltd., Ferndale). 4) Rovi, the card magician d.1996 is called the 'Welsh Wizard' in an obituary (Yr Enfys, Summer 1996, p.18). Rori was an international entertainer and the first Welshman to be made President of the International Brotherhood of Magicians. 5) Harri Webb (b.1920), poet. In his capacity of editor of the WELSH REPUBLICAN MOVEMENT'S newspaper he has been referred to as 'Wizard Webb' (Gwer. 1996:139). 6) G. Evans writes of Owain Glyndŵr, the WELSH REBEL HERO (qv.). 'The wizard vanished from the sight of the Welsh and English alike' (1988:138). 7) Literally the epithet 'Welsh Wizard' can be applied to famous Welsh magicians like Merlin (Myrrdin) and Gwydion etc. cf. Sir Walter Scott who is the Wizard of the North. 8) The 'Leekes Welsh Wizards' won the British Squash League Championship in 1990, 1992 and 1994.

**Welshwoman** (Cymraes): Can be written as one word. As the word WELSMAN, the Welsh equivalent is also one word.

**Welshwomen** (Cymraesau): Plural of WELSHWOMAN. Also one word or two.

**Welsh Women's Society:** Merched y Wawr ('Daughters of the Dawn').

**Welsh-won:** Won (or taken) by the Welsh. Kirk writes that copper and granite were 'landed from overseas at lower cost than the Welsh-won materials' (1994:164).

**Welsh Wonders, The Seven:** Or more commonly The Seven Wonders of Wales: The Mountains of Snowdon, Churchyard of Overton, bells of Gresford Church, Bridge of Llangollen,

Wrexham steeple (really a tower), waterfall at Pistyll Rhaeadr, St Winefride's Well, Holywell (see WELSH LOURDES). Also by analogy with the great Seven Wonders of the World. There are 7 wonders in Wiltshire; the Isle of Wight (as a tourism poster showed in the film *Something to Hide* with Peter Finch); and 7 Wonders of Fore (in Ireland – see O'Farrell 1978:82-3).

**Welsh Wonder Tales:** A category of Welsh legends (see Barnes 1991).

**Welsh wool:** The wool from WELSH SHEEP (qv.).

**'Welsh woollen tweed':** See WELSH TWEED.

**Welsh woollen whittle:** Part of WELSH COSTUME.

**'Welsh woolmark label':** M.E. Jones tells us that 'Along with the established woolmark, there is a special Welsh woolmark label bearing the Red Dragon of Wales' (1978:27).

**'Welsh wool smock':** Unique type of Welsh smock made of wool (M.E. Jones 1978:7).

**'Welsh-word':** Or 'wealh word' was a 'wanton word' and derived from the Anglo Saxon 'wealian' – 'to be impudent, bold or wanton' (J. Green 1996:92).

**'Welshworld':** One word. Mark Jenkins writes 'Welshness is becoming a virtual reality helmet, with a software called 'Welshworld' . . . ' (NWR 30:75-6, Autumn 1995).

**'Welsh World No.1 Golfer':** As Ian Woosnam, M.B.E. is called (Yr Enfys, Spring 1992:4).

**Welsh-woven:** (Of wool etc.) woven in Wales. Drawing an analogy with Gandhi's concept of 'Swadeshi' (helping support local products) Gwynfor Evans writes that leader of the WELSH COLONY Michael D. Jones 'wore Welsh-woven clothes, not only in order to identify himself with the people, but, more importantly, to help give work to Welsh people' (1988:266).

**Welsh wrestling** (Ymaflyd Codwm Cymreig): A unique form of wrestling distinct from catch. It is very similar in form to 'Cornish wrestling' (Corn. dial 'wrasslin' and in Corn. lang.

'gwrynya' vb.) and in Brittany 'La Lutte Bretonne' (Bret. goueren), and to a lesser extent to Cumberland wrestling. 'Welsh wrestling' has a much smaller following than its sister forms in Cornwall etc. and friendly matches have been arranged between Welsh wrestlers and Cornish or Breton opponents (see ap Dafydd 1985:16-17). cf. WELSH HOCKEY, WELSH POLO.

**Welsh-writing:** (Adj.) Refers to someone who writes in Welsh. In a speech 28th Oct. 1946 (and again at the WELSH DAY DEBATE, 12th Dec. 1953) Aneurin Bevan talked of 'Welsh-speaking, Welsh-writing zealots'.

**Welsh-wrought:** (Of iron etc.) wrought in Wales. cf. WELSH METHOD.

**Welsh Wye:** Eg. Condry writes 'Take that line down the Welsh Wye from Rhayader' (1993:20). This refers to the Welsh stretch of the Wye or perhaps a Welsh equivalent of the Wye in terms of beauty (since Rhayader is nearer the Elan Valley than the Wye Valley).

**Welsh Xanadu:** By allusion to Coleridge's mystical place in 'kubla khan', Wynford Vaughan Thomas (1981:134) describes Portmeirion as Sir Clough Williams-Ellis' 'Welsh Xanadu' (see also WELSH PORTOFINO). Less commonly it is called eg. by Dewi Roberts the 'Xanadu of Wales' (BWA. No.48:9, July '97). There are other connections between Wales and Xanadu: Coleridge was believed to have been a visitor at Thomas Johnes' home of Hafod Ychtryd in the Ystwyth Valley and 'may have had it in mind when writing of Xanadu' (Stephens ed.1986:295). Gerald Morgan gives the title 'Letters from Xanadu' to his review of Richard J. Moore-Colyer's (ed.) *A Land of Pure Delight: Selections from the Letters of Thomas Johnes of Hafod 1784-1816* (Planet 96:100-2, Dec./Jan. 1992-3). Similarly a walking tour in N. Wales with his friend John Hucks, inspired John Livingston Lowes to write his book 'Road to Xanadu' (esp. pp. 209-13). cf. WELSH EDEN, WELSH ELDORADO, WELSH GARDEN OF EDEN etc.

**Welshy:** 1) Cymreigaidd – WELSH-LIKE. 2) A WELSHPERSON. cf. Taffy, Manxy etc.

**Welsh yard:** Forty inches (see J. Geraint Evans 1976:75). A 'pren llathen' was a yardstick used to measure; approx. half a yard was a 'cyfelin' – 18 inches, 'cwart' was a quarter of a yard, a 'canllath' 100 yards. Similarly a 'beriau' was an old four foot measure (G.P.C., p.274). A Welsh proverb says 'Os caiff y Sais llathaid, fe gymer filltir' (give an Englishman a yard and he'll take a mile). cf. A Manx yard 37½ inches, Scottish yard or 'Scots ell' – 37 inches, etc. See WELSH ACRE, WELSH MILE.

**'Welsh yarn':** Of WELSH WOOL and dyed with natural colours (eg. Etheridge 1990:52).

**'Welsh year':** As Freeman calls the old calendar, 12 days later (1984:4), still used for celebration of some folk customs.

**'Welsh Yeast Cake:** A unique Welsh recipe for which the fruit is first soaked in tea (Smith-Twiddy 1979:64).

**Welsh yellow poppies:** The WELSH POPPIES (qv.) identical in shape to the red but a soft yellow colour.

**Welsh Yes Men:** With reference to the Welsh people who voted for WELSH DEVOLUTION, the headlines of The South Wales Echo scathingly wrote 'It's the D-Day Massacre of the Welsh Yes-Men' (Friday, March 2, 1979). Yet many would argue the opposite!

**Welshyish:** A bit WELSHY.

**'Welshy-Welsh':** Stereotype category of WELSH PEOPLE. Phrase quoted in NWR (37:13, 1997 and 39:38, 1997-98).

**Welsh yuppies:** Wuppies.

**Welsh 'Z':** It doesn't exist. There is no 'z' in the Welsh alphabet and 's' is used for words such as 'sero' (zero) and 'sw' (zoo).

# Bibliography:

Aaron, Jane, *A National Seduction: Wales in Nineteenth Century Women's Writing*, NWR 27:31-8, Winter 1994-95

Abse, Leo, *A Tale of Collaboration not Conflict with The People of The Book*, NWR 22:16-21, Autumn 1993

Alford, Violet, *The Hobby Horse and Other Animal Marks*, (The Merlin Press, London 1978)

Alsopp, Richard, *Dictionary of Carribean English Usage*, (Oxford University Press, 1996)

Andrew, William (ed.), *Old Church Life . . .* , (1900, pub. author)

ap Dafydd, Myrddin, *Ymaflyd Codwm Cymreig*, pp.16-17 from 'Llafar Gwlad', No.7, 1985

ap Dafydd, Myrddin, *Enwau Tafarnau Cymru*, (Llyfrau 'Llafar Gwlad' 9, Gwasg Carreg Gwalch, 1988)

ap Huw, Alwyn, *Welsho yn Saesneg*, p.11 from 'Llafar Gwlad' No.50, 1995

Ayto, John, *A Gourmets Guide: Food and Drink from A to Z*, (Oxford University Press, 1994)

Baines, Anthony, *The Oxford Companion to Musical Instruments*, (Oxford, 1992)

Baker, Margaret, *Discovering The Folklore of Plants*, (Shire Publications Ltd. 1996)

Baker, Simon, *Imagined Homelands: The Welsh Story in English*, pp.8-10 from 'Books in Wales', Winter 1995

Balsom, Denis (ed.) *The Wales Yearbook, 1996* (H.T.V. 1996)

Barber, Chris, *The Seven Hills of Abergavenny*, (Blorenge Books, Abergavenny, 1992)

Barnes, Ronald, *Great Legends of Wales*, (Colin Smythe, Gerrards Cross, 1991)

Basini, Mario, *Lime, Lemon and Internment*, pp.58-60, NWR 16, 1992

Bebb, Richard, *Welsh Country Furniture*, (Shire Publications Ltd. 1994)

Beedell, Suzanne & Hargreaves, Barbara, *The Complete Guide to Country Living*, (David & Charles, Newton Abbot, London, 1979)

Bennet, Richard, *Howard Harris and the Dawn of Revival*, (1962, rep. Evangelical Press of Wales, 1987)

Berlitz, Charles, *Native Tongues,* (Granada, London, 1983)

Bogle, Joanna, *A Book of Feasts and Seasons,* (Fowler Wright Books, Leominster 1988)

Borrow, George, *Wild Wales: Its People, Language and Scenery,* (1862, rep. Thomas Nelson and Sons, no date)

Bowie, Fiona & Oliver Davies (eds.), *Discovering Welshness* (Gomer, 1992)

Boycott, Rosie, *Batty, Bloomers and Boycott,* (Hutchinson, 1982)

Brears, Peter C.D., *The Knitting Sheath,* pp.16-40 from 'Folk Life' 20, 1981-2

Briggs, Katherine, *A Dictionary of Fairies,* (1976, Penguin 1979)

Bromwich, Rachel, *Trioedd Ynys Prydein/The Welsh Triads,* (1961, University of Wales Press, 2nd ed.1991)

Brown, John, *Welsh Stick Chairs,* (Abercastle, 1990)

Carpenter, Humphrey & Mari Prichard, *The Oxford Companion to Children's Literature,* (Oxford, 1984)

Carr, A.D., *The Historical Background, 1282-1550* pp.11-35 from A.O.H. Jarman & Gwilym Rees Hughes (eds.), 'A Guide to Welsh Literature', Vol.2. (Christopher Davies, Llandybïe 1979, 2nd imp. 1984)

Charles, Edward, T.M., *The Welsh Laws,* (University of Wales Press, Cardiff, 1989)

Clark, Thomas L., *Western Lore and Language* (University of Utah Press, Salt Lake City, 1996)

Clews, Roy, *To Dream of Freedom,* (Y Lolfa, 1980)

Colfey, Andrew, *Welsh Adventurers* (Vantage Press, New York, 1981)

Collins, Marie & Pownall Deborah (Picture Research), *Caxton: The Description of Britain: A Modern Rendering,* (Weidenfield & Nicolson, N.Y., 1988)

Colyer, Richard, *Roads and Trackways of Wales,* (Moorland Publishing, Ashbourne, Derbyshire, 1984)

Condry, William, *A Welsh Country Diary* (Gomer, 1993)

Couch, Jonathan, *The History of Polperro,* (1871, rep. Dyllansow Truran, Redruth, 1965)

Davies, D. Hywel, *South Wales History which Excludes The Welsh,* N.W.R. 26:8-13, Autumn 1994

Davies, Jonathan Caredig, *Folk-lore of West and Mid-Wales*, (1911, rep. Llanerch, 1992)

Davies, T.A., *Folklore of Gwent* from 'Folklore', Vol.XLVIII, March 1937

Davies, Tom, *Tiger Bay and The Law of Love*, N.W.R. 15:26-9, Winter 1991-92

Davies, Wynne, *An Introduction to Welsh Ponies and Cobs* (Whittet Books, London, 1993)

Davies, John (golygydd), *Cymru'n Deffro: Hanes y Blaid Genedlaethol 1925-75* (Y Lolfa, 1981)

De Camp, L. Sprague, *Lost Continents: The Atlantis Theme in History, Science and Literature* (1954, Dover Publications, New York, 1970)

Dixon-Kennedy, Mike, *Celtic Myth and Legend* (Blandford, 1997)

Dyebr, T.F. Thistleton, *Church-lore Gleanings*, (A.D. Innes & Co. 1892)

Edwards, Gillian, *Hob goblin and Sweet Puck: Fairy Names and Natures*, (Geoffrey Bades, London, 1974)

Edwards, Hywel Teifi, *The Eisteddfod*, (University of Wales Press, Cardiff, 1990)

Edwards, John, *Talk Tidy: The Art of Speaking Wenglish* (D. Brown & Sons Ltd., Cowbridge, 1985)

Elias, Twm, *Y Porthmyn Cymreig*, (Gwasg Carreg Gwalch, 1987)

Ellis, Alice Thomas (ed.), *Wales: An Anthology*, (Fontana, 1989, rep. 1991)

Ellis, Osian, *The Story of the Harp in Wales*, (University of Wales Press, 1991)

Ellis, Peter Berresford, *The Celtic Revolution*, (Y Lolfa, 1985, 2nd imp. 1988)

Ellis, Peter Berresford, *Dictionary of Celtic Mythology*, (Constable, 1992)

Emmett, Isabel, *A North Wales Village* (R.K.P., London, 1964)

Etheridge, Ken, *Welsh Costume in the 18th and 19th Century*, (Christopher Davies, Llandybïe, Dyfed, 1990)

Evans, Gwynfor, *Welsh Nation Builders*, (Gomer, 1988)

Evans, Gwynfor, *Fighting for Wales*, (Y Lolfa, 1991)

Evans, Gwynfor, *For the Lake of Wales* (trans. Meic Stephens) (Welsh Academic Press, 1996)

Evans, Gwynfor, *Land of My Fathers* (1974, Y Lolfa, 3rd paperback impression 1993)

Evans, R. Wallis, *Prophetic Poetry*, pp.276-97 from A.O.H. Jarman & Gwilym Rees Hughes (eds.) *A Guide to Welsh Literature*, Vol.2. (Christopher Davies, Llandybïe, 1979, 2nd imp. 1984)

Fishlock, Trevor, Review of William D. Jones', *Wales in America*, N.W.R. 22:72-3, Autumn 1993

*Folklore of Blaenau, Gwent* (Old Bakehouse Publications, Abertillery, 1995)

Frankenberg, Ronald, *Village on the Border: A Social Study of Religion, Politics and Football in a North Wales Community* (Waveland Press Inc., Prospect Heights, Illinois, 1957, reissued with changes, 1990)

Freeman, Bobby, *A Book of Welsh Country Cakes and Buns*, (Y Lolfa, 1984)

Freeman, Bobby, *Welsh Country Cookery: Traditional Recipes from The Country Kitchen of Wales*, (Y Lolfa, Talybont, 1988)

Freeman, Bobby, *A Book of Welsh Bread* (Y Lolfa, 1981, rep.1993)

Freeman, B., *A Book of Welsh Bakestone Cookery* (Y Lolfa, 1984, rep.1991)

Freeman, B., *A Book of Welsh Country Puddings and Pies* (Y Lolfa, 1984, rep.1993)

Freeman, B., *First Catch your Peacock* (Y Lolfa, revised paperback edition, 1996)

Fynes-Clinton, O.H., *The Welsh Vocabulary of the Bangor District*, (2 vols.) 1913 (facsimile rep. Llanerch 1995)

Garlick, Raymon, *An Introduction to Anglo-Welsh Literature*, (University of Wales Press, 1970, rep. 1972)

Gater, Dilys, *The Battles of Wales*, (Gwasg Carreg Gwalch, 1991)

George, Siwsan & Brown, Stuart & Meazey, Peter, *Mabsant* (Y Lolfa, 1980)

G.F.W.I. (Gwent Federation of Women's Institutes), *The Gwent Village Book*, (GFWI & Countryside Books, Newbury & Usk, 1994)

Glam. W.F.I., *The Glamorgan Village Book* (pub. jointly by Countryside Books, Newbury and the Glamorgan Federation of Women's Institutes, 1993)

Grant, Chris, *Welsh Country Cooking*, (Gwasg Carreg Gwalch, 1993)

Green, Jonathan, *Words Apart: The Language of Prejudice* (Kyle Cathie Ltd., London, 1996)

Green, Miranda J., *Dictionary of Celtic Myth and Legend*, (Thames and

Hudson, 1992)

Grenfell-Hill, Jeffrey, *Growing Up in Wales 1895-1939* (Gomer, Llandysul, 1996)

Griffiths, Gwyn, *Goodbye, Johnny Onions*, (Dyllansow Truran, Redruth, 1987)

Grimes, Dorothy A., *Like Dew Before the Sun*, (Rushden, 1991)

'Gweriniaethwr', *The Young Republicans*, (Gwasg Carreg Gwalch, 1996)

Gwyndaf, Robin, *Welsh Folk Tales*, (Welsh Folk Museum, Cardiff, 1989)

Gwyndaf, Robin, *Welsh Tradition-Bearers: Guidelines for the Study of World-view*, pp.77-91 from *Folk Life*, Vol.32, 1993-94.

Haining, Peter, *A Dictionary of Ghosts*, (Robert Hale, London, 1982)

Harris, Mary Corbett, *Crafts, Customs and Legends of Wales*, (David & Charles, 1980)

Harrison, Paul, *South Wales Murder Casebook* (Countryside Books, Newbury)

Hazlitt, W.C., *Dictionary of Faiths and Folklore: Beliefs, Superstitions and Popular Customs*, (1905, Bracken Books, London, 1995)

Hearne, Derrick, *The ABC of The Welsh Revolution*, (Y Lolfa, 1982)

Hearne, Derrick, *The Joy of Freedom* (Y Lolfa, 1977)

Hendrickson, Robert, *Animal Crackers: A Bestial Lexicon*, (Viking Press/Penguin Books, New York, 1983)

Herbert, Trevor & Gareth Elwyn Jones (eds.), *Edward I and Wales* (University of Wales Press, 1988)

Herbert, Trevor & Gareth Elwyn Jones (eds.) *Post War Wales* (University Press of Wales, 1995)

Hickey, D.J. & J.E. Doherty, *A Dictionary of Irish History 1800-1980*, (Gill and Macmillan 1980, Dublin, rep. 1987)

Hodgson, Bryan, *Wales: The Lyric Land*, pp.36-62 from National Geographic, Vol.164, No.1, July 1983

Hole, Christina, *A Dictionary of British Folk Customs*, (1976, Granada pub. Ltd. 1978, London)

Holland, Richard (ed.), *Bye-gones*, (Gwasg Carreg Gwalch, 1992)

Hosier, F. Audrey, *The Measured Mile* pp.544-556 from Old Cornwall, Vol.IX, No.11, Autumn 1984

Howells, Sheila, *Favourite Welsh Recipes* (J. Salmon Ltd., Sevenoaks)

Hughes, Meirion & Evans, Wayne, *Rumours and Oddities from North*

*Wales*, (Gwasg Carreg Gwalch, 1986, 2nd ed. 1995)

Humphreys, Emyr, *The Taliesin Tradition: A Quest for the Welsh Identity*, (Black Raven Press, London, 1983)

Humphreys, Jonathan & Bennet, Andrew, *Capten Cymru* (Y Lolfa, 1996)

Hutton, Ronald, *The Stations of The Sun: A History of the Ritual Year in Britain* (Oxford University Press, 1996)

Isaacs, Alan & Jonathan Law (eds.), *Brewer's Dictionary of 20th Century Phrase and Fable* (1991, Cassell, 1994)

Jackson, Sara, *Methodism and Mining*, pp.37-43 from Brian Bell (ed.), *Insight Guides: Wales*, (A.P.A. Publications, 1989)

Jeffrey, P.H., *Ghosts, Legends and Lore of Wales* (The Old Orchard Press, Cambridge, no date)

Jenkins, Geraint H., *Tis a Tongue not made for every mouth: The Welsh Language*, pp.8-10 from 'The Celtic History Review', Vol.2, Issue 2, Spring 1996

Jenkins, John, *Prison Letters*, (Y Lolfa, 1981)

Jenkins, J. Geraint, *Life and Tradition in Rural Wales*, (1976, Alan Sutton, Wolfbura Falls, 1992)

Jenkins, J. Geraint, *The Coracle*, (Golden Grove, Carmarthen, 1988)

Jenkins, J. Geraint, *Exploring Museums: Wales*, (1990, London, HMSO)

Jenkins, J. Geraint, *From Fleece To Fabric* (Gomer, 1981)

Jenkins, J. Geraint, *The Flannel Makers: A Brief History of the Welsh Woollen Industry* (Gomer)

John, Brian S., *Rural Crafts of Wales*, (Green Croft Books, Newport, 1976)

Johnston, Dafydd, *A Pocket Guide: The Literature of Wales* (Cardiff University of Wales Press, 1994)

Jones, Alison, *Larousse Dictionary of World Folklore*, (Larousse, Edinburgh, 1995)

Jones, Anna M., *The Rural Industries of England and Wales* (Vol.4), (Oxford University Press, 1927, republished E.P. Publishing, East Ardsley, W. Yorkshire 1978)

Jones, Bob Griff & Owen, Meurig, *Ways with Hazel and Horn*, (1996, Gwasg Carreg Gwalch)

Jones, David, *The Tenby Daffodil: The Remarkable Story of The True Welsh*

*Daffodil* (The Tenby Museum, 1992)

Jones, Glanville R.J., *The Models for Organisation in 'Llyfr Iorwerth' and 'Llyfr Cyfnerth'*, pp.95-118 from 'The Bulletin of The Board of Celtic Studies', Vol.XXXIX, 1992/University of Wales Press)

Jones, Gwyn, *Welsh Legends and Folk Tales*, (Oxford 1951, Puffin Classics, 1970)

Jones, Gwyn, Islwyn Ffowc Elis (eds.), *Classic Welsh Short Stories*, (Oxford, 1971, rep. 1992)

Jones, J. Graham, *A Pocket Guide to the History of Wales*, (Cardiff, University of Wales Press, 1990)

Jones, John, *Recipes from Wales* (John Jones Publishing Ltd., Cardiff, 1994)

Jones, Lewis, *The Chapel*, pp.63-5 from Brian Bell (ed.) 'Insight Guide: Wales' (APA, 1989)

Jones, Margaret, *Eisteddfod: A Welsh Phenomenon*, (Aberaeron, 1986)

Jones, Mary Eirwen, *Welsh Crafts*, (B.T. Butsford, London, 1978)

Jones, Noragh, *Living in Rural Wales* (Gomer, 1993)

Jones, T. Gwynn, *Welsh Folklore and Folk-Custom*, (1930, 1979, D.S. Brewer, Cambridge)

Joyce, P.W., *English As We Speak it in Ireland*, (1910, rep. Wolfhound Press, Dublin, 1991)

Kerr, Alex, *Lost Japan*, (Lonely Planet, Australia, 1993)

Kindersley, Doring, *The Royal Horticultural Society Encyclopaedia of Gardening* (1992)

Kirk, David, *Snowdonia: A Historical Anthology*, (Gwasg Carreg Gwalch, 1994)

Lambeth, M., *Discovering Corn Dollies*, (Shire Publications, Ltd. 1974, rep. 1984)

Leach, Maria (ed.), *Funk and Wagnalls Standard Dictionary of Folklore, Mythology and Legend*, (1949, rep. Harper and Row, 1984)

Lewis, Jacqueline, *Passing Judgements: Welsh Dress and The English Tourist*, pp.29-47 from 'Folk Life', Vol.33, 1994-95.

Llanover, Lady, *Good Cooking Illustrated: And Recipes Communicated by The Welsh Hermit of The Cell of St Gover* (Richard Bentley, London, 1867)

Llewellyn, Sian, *Customs and Cooking from Wales*, (Esmerelda Ltd.,

Cardiff, 1974, rep. 1977)

Lloyd, Bertram, *Notes on Pembrokeshire Folk-lore, Superstitions, Dialect Words etc.* pp. 307-20 from 'Folklore' 56 (1945)

Lloyd, Sir J.E., *Owen Glendower (Owain Glyndŵr)* (1931, Oxford, rep. Llanerch, 1992)

Lofmark, Carl (ed. G.A. Wells), *A History of The Red Dragon,* (Gwasg Carreg Gwalch, 1995)

Lowes, John Livingston, *The Road to Xanadu,* (Constable, London, 1930)

Macafee, C.I., *A Concise Ulster Dictionary* (Oxford University Press, 1996)

MacDonald Junior Reference library: Heraldry (1970, 2nd imp. 1974)

McArthur, Tom (ed.), *The Oxford Companion to the English Language,* (Oxford 1992)

Magda, Matthew S., *The Welsh in Pennsylvania* (Pennsylvania Historical and Museum Commission, 1986)

Mathias, Roland, *Anglo-Welsh Literature: An Illustrated History,* (Poetry Wales Press, Bridgend, 1987)

Matthews, John & Caitlin, *British and Irish Mythology: An Encyclopaedia of Myth and Legend,* (The Aquarian Press, Harper Collins, 1988)

Maud, Ralph, *Guide to Welsh Wales* (Y Lolfa, 1994)

May, John, *Reference Wales* (University of Wales Press, 1994)

Miles, Dilwyn (ed.), George Owen of Henllys *The Description of Pembrokeshire* (Welsh Classics, Vol.6, Gomer, 1994)

Miles, John, *Princes and People of Wales,* (1969, rep. The Starling Press, Risca, 1977)

Miller, Judith & Martin, *Millers' Pocket Dictionary of Antiques,* (Michael Beazley, London 1990)

Mills, A.D., *The Popular Dictionary of English Place-Names* (1991, Parragon Book Service Ltd., imprint of Oxford University Press, 1996)

Morgan, Kenneth O., *Modern Wales: Politics, Place and People',* (University of Wales, 1995)

Morgan, Moc, *Trout and Salmon Flies of Wales* (Merlin, Unwin Books, Ludlow, 1996)

Moore, Chas, *C.B. Language: The Complete Dictionary of Truckers Talk,* (W.H. Allen & Co., 1981)

Morris, Jan, *The Princeship of Wales* (From series 'Changing Wales', Meic Stephens, ed., Gomer, 1995)

Morris, W. Meredith, *A Glossary of The Demetian Dialect*, (Tonypandy 1910, Llanerch 1991)

O'Farrell, Padraic, *Superstitions of the Irish Country People*, (The Mercier Press, Cork/Dublin, 1978, rep. 1991)

Owen, Elias, *Welsh Folklore: A Collection of Folk-tales and Legends of North Wales*, (Prize essay of the National Eisteddfod, 1887, Llanerch, 1996)

Owen, Trefor M., *Welsh Folk Customs*, (National Museum of Wales, 1959, rep. 1978)

Owen, Trefor M., *A Pocket Guide: The Customs and Traditions of Wales*, (University of Wales Press)

Padel, O.J., *Two New Pre-Conquest Charters for Cornwall*, pp.20-7 from 'Cornish Studies', Vol.6, 1978

Palfrey, Colin & Roberts, Arwel, *The Unofficial Guide to Wales* (Y Lolfa 1994, 2nd imp. 1995)

Palmer, Roy, *The Folklore of Gloucestershire* (West Country Books, Tiverton, 1994)

Parker, Mike and Paul Whitfield, *Wales: The Rough Guide* (1997)

Parry-Jones, D., *Welsh Children's Games and Pastimes*, (Gee & Son Ltd., Denbigh, 1964)

Parry-Jones, D., *Welsh Country Characters*, (The Ffynnon Press, 1952, rep. 1973)

Partridge, Eric, *The Penguin Dictionary of Historical Slang*, (1972, rep. 1988)

Payton, Philip, *Cornwall*, (Alexander Associates, 1996)

Peate, Iorwerth C., *Mari Lwyd – Láir Bhán*, pp.95-6 from 'Folk Life', Vol.1, 1963

Peate, Iorwerth C., *Tradition and Folk Life: A Welsh View*, (Faber & Faber, 1972)

Peel, Hazel M., *Pocket Dictionary of the Horse*, (Abson Books, Bristol, 1978)

Petro, Pamela J., *Welsh Athens of America*, Review of Williams D. Jones' 'Wales in America: Scranton and the Welsh 1860-1920' pp.107-8, Planet 105, June/July 1994

Piehler, H.A., *Wales for Everyman* (J.M. Dent and Sons Ltd., London 1935, rep. 1939)

Plomer, William (ed.), *Kilvert's Diary: Selections from the Diary of the Reverend Francis Kilvert 1870-1879* (1944, Book Club Associates, 1978, London)

Pope, Clive Mason, *A-Z of Staffordshire Figures: A Potted History* (1990, Antique Collectors Club, Woodbridge, rep. 1996)

Pugh, Jane, *Welsh Ghostly Encounters*, (1990, Gwasg Carreg Gwalch, Llanrwst)

Readers Digest Great Encyclopaedia Dictionary in Three Volumes, The (The Readers Digest Association, London, Montreal & Cape Town, 1965)

Rees, Alwyn D., *Life in a Welsh Countryside: A Social Study of Llanfihangel yng Ngwynfa* (1950, rep. University of Wales Press, 1996)

Renouard, M. et al., *Dictionnaire de Bretagne*, (Éditions Ouest-France, 1992)

Rhy, John, *Celtic Folklore: Welsh and Manx* (2 Vols, 1901)

Richards, John Winterson, *The Xenophobes' Guide to the Welsh*, (Ravette Books, London, 1993)

Roberts, Mair, *Seiri Telyn Cymru*, (Gwasg Carreg Gwalch, 1992)

Roberts, Peter, *The Cambrian Popular Antiquities of Wales*, (1815, rep. Library and Information Service, Mold, Clwyd, 1994)

Roberts, Tony, *Myths and Legends of Wales*, (1984, rep. Dynefor Press, Llandybïe, 1991)

Roderick, Alan, *The Folklore of Glamorgan*, (Village Publishing, Cwmbrân, 1986)

Roderick, Alan, *The Newport Kaleidoscope* (Handpost Books, Newport, 1994)

Rollinson, William, *Life and Tradition in the Lake District*, (1987, Dalesman Books, Clapham via Lancaster)

Rosser, David, *A Dragon in the House* (Gomer, 1987)

Sanders, T.W., *The Encyclopaedia of Gardening* (W.H. & L. Collingride, Aldersgate, no date)

Searby, Peter, *The Chartists in Wales*, (Longman, 1986)

Senior, Michael, *Disputed Border*, (Gwasg Carreg Gwalch, Llanrwst, 1989)

Sikes, Wirt, *British Goblins: The Realm of Faerie*, (1880, rep. Llanerch, 1991)

Simpson, Jacqueline, *The Folklore of The Welsh Border*, (Batsford, 1976)

Sinclair, Neil M.C., *The Tiger Bay Story* (BKAP, 1993)

Smeeth, Christine, *The Welsh Table* (Y Lolfa, 1994)

Smith, Graham, *Headlines from South Wales* (Countryside Books, Newbury, 1993)

Smith, Muriel, W.G., *National Apple Register* (M.A.F.F. 1971)

Smith-Twiddy, Helen, *Celtic Cookbook*, (Y Lolfa, 1979, 6th imp. 1989)

Stephens, Meic (ed.), *The Oxford Companion to the Literature of Wales*, (Oxford, 1986)

Stephens, Meic (ed.), *A Most Peculiar People: Quotations about Wales and the Welsh*, (Cardiff, University of Wales Press, 1992)

Stevens, Catrin, *The Funeral Wake in Wales*, pp.27-45 from 'Folk Life', Vol.14, 1976

Stevens, Catrin, *Welsh Courting Customs*, (Gomer, 1993)

Stickings, Thomas F., *The Story of Saundersfoot*, (H.G. Walters, Tenby 1970, rep. 1976)

Sutton, Ann, *The Textiles of Wales*, (Bellew Publishing Company Limited, 1987)

Thomas, Roger, *A Journey Through Wales*, (Jarrold, Norwich, 1990)

Thompson, R.W., *An Englishman Looks at Wales*, (Arrowsmith, 1937)

Thurner, Dick, *Portmanteau Dictionary*, (McFarland and Company, Inc. Jefferson, N. Carolina, 1993)

Tibbott, S. Minwel, *Geirfa'r Gegin*, (Amgueddfa Werin Cymru, 1983)

Trosset, Carol, *Welshness Performed: Welsh Concepts of Person and Society* (The University of Arizona Press, Tucson, Arizona, 1993)

Tucker, Anna, *Gwent*, (Shire County Guide, 1987)

Tudur, Gwilym (ed.), *Wyt ti'n Cofio?* (Y Lolfa, 1989)

Unsworth, Walt, *Encyclopaedia of Mountaineering*, (1975, Pub. Penguin, 1977)

Vaughan-Thomas, Wynford, *Wales*, (Mermaid 1981, 4th imp. 1986)

Villiers, Alan, *Wales: Land of Bards*, pp.727-69 from National Geographic, Vol.127, No.6, June 1965

Voth, Norma Jost, *Festive Breads of Christmas,* (Herald Press, Scottdale, Pennsylvania, 1983)

Walkley, Christina, *Welcome Sweet Babe: A Book of Christenings* (Peter Owen, London, 1987)

Wall, Richard, *An Anglo-Irish Dialect Dictionary for Joyce's Works,* (Syracuse University Press, New York, 1987)

Waller, Betty, *Granny's Kitchen,* (Whistlestop, Calstock, Cornwall, 1994)

Waring, Philippa, *A Dictionary of Omens and Superstitions,* (Magnum Books, London, 1978)

Wedeck, H.E., *Dictionary of Gipsy Life and Lore,* (Peter Owen, London, 1973)

Welsh Pony and Cob Society Journal, The (1991) (Welsh Pony and Cob Society, Aberystwyth)

Wilde, Sir William R., *Irish Popular Superstitions* (Sterling Publishing Co.Inc., NY. 1995)

Wiliam, Eurwyn, *Welsh Long-houses,* (University of Wales Press, Cardiff, 1992)

Williams, David, *Cymru ac America/Wales and America,* (University of Wales, 1975)

Williams, Glyn, *The Welsh in Patagonia,* (University of Wales Press, Cardiff, 1991)

Williams, Jac L., *Geiriadur Termau/Dictionary of Terms,* (University of Wales Press, 1973)

Williams, James, *Give me Yesterday* (Country Book Club, Newton Abbot, 1973)

Williams, Margaret, *The Smallest House Cook Book,* (Gwasg Carreg Gwalch, 1992)

Wilson, John, *The Chicago of Wales,* pp.14-25 from Planet 115, Feb./March 1996)

Woodhouse, Harry, *Cornish Bagpipes: Fact or Fiction?* (Dyllansow Truran, Redruth, 1994)

Wright, Peter, *Cumbrian Chat,* (Dalesman, Clapham via Lancaster, 1989)